kavet's internet sites

for your Wedding *and* Honeymoon

PUBLISHED BY

BOSTON AMERICA CORP.

www.bostonamerica.com

125 WALNUT STREET, WATERTOWN, MASSACHUSETTS 02472

TEL: (617) 923 1111 • FAX: (617) 923 8839

KAVET'S INTERNET SITES FOR YOUR WEDDING AND HONEYMOON: ISBN 1-889647-55-1. PRINTED IN U.S.A.

Written by Herbert I. Kavet

Edited by Karen Kavet

Designed by Victoria Bocash of *Inktree Design*

Contributions by Mimi Cail of *Consultations*

dedication...

To my wife Karen who taught me to use a computer, unraveled all my crashes, helped immeasurably with the research and converted all my ramblings into correct English.

thank you...

Also, with thanks to Mimi Cail, of Consultations, Concord MA wedding consultant and event planner, for her valuable advice and suggestions and to Victoria Bocash of Inktree Design for her design and art direction.

Table of Contents

table of contents

Introduction

Planning a wedding is a serious and complex enterprise and you are going to need all the help you can get. This book can make the job easier by putting hundreds of internet sites that provide information and ideas at your fingertips. Sure, you can find all these places yourself. But, this book will save you hours of hunting and surfing and make it faster and easier to find services you need and may even provide a few that you wouldn't have thought of by yourself. The more information you have, the easier the planning will be and the more elegant or economical the outcome. (Except in shopping for your dress. If you bring more than your mother and one friend along you are just asking for trouble.)

Apology and Disclaimer...

When I wrote this book all the sites listed were live and available. When you go to some of them, you'll find they've disappeared. God only knows where they go. Some will disappear and some will come back an hour later and some will somehow evolve into a site for Korean folk remedies translated into Hungarian. The internet is indeed a mysterious place. My best advice, if this happens, is to simply move on to the next site. There are plenty listed in each category and since most of them are anxious to sell you something, my guess is they will be available longer than some teenager's homesite.

Many entrepreneurs are trying to get rich using the internet and many of the sites in this book, especially those promising nationwide sources for things like photographers or wedding consultants, are still in the developing stage. Some of these sites are a disappointment at present but may get better if they don't go out of business first.

The publishers and distributors of this book cannot take responsibility for what you find or don't find or what these sites lead you to or what you may buy and then get stuck with or absolutely love or any other of the fascinating or frustrating and endless paths of the internet. I mean, don't blame me if the crystal breaks, the favors have worms in them or the honeymoon suite bed creaks.

How To Use This Book

Most of the internet sites listed provide wedding information or products like gowns or accessories or favors or china that can be easily bought by mail order. It's harder to use this guide to find a site for your reception or a caterer or an official or even a consultant. While some sites claim to provide vendors throughout the country, in truth, most are just starting or trying to build their networks and haven't quite gotten to the point of having a photographer in Poughkeepsie or a caterer in Watertown. These local venders will be much better represented in local yellow pages or newspaper wedding supplements than in any site purporting to cover the entire country. This book's main function is to save you time by exposing you to gown choices and in hunting for secondary needs like cake tops or original vows, or flower preservers or online invitations and to show you where to find information on honeymoon sites and etiquette questions.

I've left out the http:// from the beginning of each address since most computers are set up to enter that automatically. And when a notice comes up saying that a site cannot be found, please check the address you typed in before cursing me out. It's real easy to make a slight typo and tiny errors fool the smartest computers.

Planning Your Wedding

I wrote this book so you could do it all yourself but just in case you get cold feet or find your computer doesn't work you can always turn to a wedding consultant. These consultants have been through it all hundreds of times and usually have a wealth of information and ideas. If you find someone on the same wavelength as you, these people can make planning the wedding a cinch. While they may charge by the hour, by flat fee, or by a percentage of the total cost, a good consultant can really save you money by knowing the right vendors, avoiding mistakes and even negotiating better prices by being able to offer repeat business to the vendors. They are also great for taking care of the last minute problems that usually arise, like torn dresses and inebriated ushers, leaving you to enjoy your day.

Wedding Consultants

www.acpwc.com

This is the site of the Association of Certified Professional Wedding Consultants. It's nice to know there is an association but unfortunately the list of their consultants is rather small.

www.weddingtips.com/wtconsul.html

A list of wedding consultants but only in California.

www.weddingtips.com/wttippr.html

A wedding consultant gives some good reasons on why to use one.

www.superweddings.com/weddingconsulting.html

A home study course in becoming a professional wedding consultant.

www.the-whole-shebang.com/pro.html

What a professional wedding coordinator can do for you.

Friends who have been recently married are one of the best sources for finding wedding consultants or you can get some names from these sites.

Wedding Magazines

Wedding magazines are the thickest, most gigantic magazines in the world. Buy two of them at a newsstand and you'll need a shopping cart to get them home. Subscribe for the year of your wedding planning, to save on the high newsstand price, and you'll learn why mail carriers get bad backs. But, these magazines are a wonderful source of ideas even if they seem to be 99% ads for gowns. The ads are probably your first extensive information source on gowns and the color pictures are breath-taking. Here are the web sites of some major magazines that are usually a smaller version of the overweight print edition.

www.modernbride.com

This magazine site has shopping, planning, chatting and all the other information that will keep you busy for months. Honeymoon planning, 100's of dresses shown by designer and even instructions on dress packing so some day your daughter might actually wear it.

tncweddings.com

Town and Country Weddings.

www.usabride.com

USABride Internet Wedding Magazine has gowns and registry and even a name change kit.

www.brides.com

All the best from Bride's Magazine including answers to the 12 most frequently asked questions.

www.weddingbells.com

A well organized online magazine that makes it easy to get started.

www.philippines1.com/abride

Asian Bride Magazine's online site with information about Asian weddings.

Wedding Networks

www.weddingnetwork.com

Tools like wedding planners, local resource guides, online registry, ideas and answers to your questions. You can find everything you need here from "Do Not Disturb" honeymoon signs to planners for managing your guest list.

www.myweddingplans.com

They advertise complete and customized wedding solutions and since they cover everything from dress previews to the top 10 honeymoon sites (plus instructions on how to pack to get there) with etiquette, planning tips, trends and receptions, they just may be correct.

fashionalley.net/wedding.htm

A great site for tips and sources of just about everything.

www.weddingzone.com

Search for your wedding and party services here as well as everything else. The top 50 wedding songs, bridal chat, free wedding planning software and much more.

These are one stop spots that will provide all the services you need for a wedding. If you and your family are experienced in wedding planning, using a packaged kind of service may take some of the excitement and sense of accomplishment out of your planning but if you "haven't a clue" it's a great place to start. Who knows, these sites may be so helpful you'll just throw away the rest of this book.

Thousands, probably millions of companies make a living selling you things for your wedding. Behind all the congratulations and offers to help lies the profit motive. Remember that many of the services offered on these networks are there because they are paying someone a commission for reaching you which may end up in higher costs for you.

Allow plenty of time to plan your wedding. Having a year may seem like loads of time when you're first engaged, but by the time you walk down the aisle you'll realize you used every day and having those months available for planning and problem solving helped keep your sanity.

The Schedule

When you first pick the date you may think you have all the time in the world. You don't. Like any complex project the time to worry about the details is at the beginning. You probably don't have to start with a panic but at least understand that the clock is ticking. Set up your schedule early and then stick to it. The site for the ceremony and reception are usually the most critical items so nail them down first. And don't forget the Clergy for the ceremony. Then look into the caterer, photographer, gown and music.

www.weddingchannel.com

Another complete wedding network with on line registration, chat rooms, gowns and hundreds of articles on every wedding subject from "Pets in Weddings" to "Soul Food On China." If you expect to read all of these you'd better plan on a very long engagement.

www.ultimateweddingmall.com

All the accessories from gifts to favors, to cameras, to garters and sweets and aisle runners and anything else you can think of.

www.wedding-world.com/coupons.html

Loads of wedding discount coupons available for your state. Perhaps you can use some of them. Check it out.

- **www.weddingweb.com**
  A well broken down list of books on wedding subjects though you will have to go to someone like Amazon to get detailed book descriptions.

- **www.weddinglane.com/cameras.html**
  Links to a zillion wedding sites in the U.S., Canada and world.

- **www.topweddingsites.com/index.html**
  The top wedding sites.

- **www.weddinglinksgalore.com**
  Links to absolutely anything you could think of needing for your wedding.

- **www.top100weddingsites.com**
  This really isn't the top 100 sites but it's a good idea and a place to find 100 miscellaneous places.

Once these wedding network sites have done a good job of intimidating you with just how much needs to be done before that wedding date (a year from now?) sit down and set up a system. You can use one of the planners shown on pages 16 and 17 or just an old notebook but keep your wedding information organized.

A good marriage usually rests upon a series of compromises. Planning a wedding will give you lots of opportunities to practice compromising and while you are practicing it's a good idea to keep a cheerful attitude about it. This learning to compromise will serve you well throughout your marriage.

www.weddingspot.com
Some good tips and information and services, like caterers, broken down by major cities.

www.1800bride2b.com
This site even gives you a run down on marriage laws which seems to be a good idea if only to make sure you're really married. Planning charts are available, the usual honeymoon stuff, budgeting, plus a free consulting service to answer your questions.

www.wedboutique.com
This site hosts a national network of "independent consultants" who'll come to your house to sell you stuff after you've sent for and paid for their catalog.

www.bridaltips.com
"Others give you fluff, we give you the stuff". A good site for tips and advice.

www.weddinglane.com
This site covers every detail of weddings that you can imagine with State by State breakdowns of local suppliers such as photographers and live music. Some locations are covered more extensively than others.

www.theknot.com
Search through 15,000 gowns and register for your gifts.

Expos

www.greatbridalexpo.com
Location and dates of Bridal Expo's around the country. These expo's are a great way to get ideas and to meet lots of local vendors at one time.

www.ultimatewedding.com
Shopping, chat rooms, resources, actually everything from poems to wedding vows to napkins and garters.

www.wednet.com
A complete store plus hundreds of articles on everything from making your own veil to alternatives to dancing for clumsy brides and grooms.

www.weddingchannel.com
A wedding resource for everything.

www.blissezine.com
Lots of the usual advice and shopping links but also good book reviews and shower games.

www.bridaltips.com
Good tips on how to avoid being taken advantage of by various wedding suppliers. And believe me, they are out there waiting for you.

If you can find a wedding expo near where you live be sure to attend. You can compare vendors very efficiently and get a quick comparison as to which are on the same wave length as you.

Wedding Planners & Software

There are loads of wedding planners in every bookstore and free wedding planners on many of the sites listed in this book. You can also download free (I think) wedding software from the following sites. Some even enable you to print your own stationery and invitations.

- www.perfectwed.com
- www.smartwedding.com/default.htm
- members.aol.com/wedsware
- www.crsoftwaresolutions.com
- www.wedsoft.com
- softrack.releasesoft.com/origin/100000/info/wedding/info.html

- **www.organizetips.com/wedhelp.htm**

  Excellent tips, some free planners and a couple of inexpensive guides for sale.

- **www.weddingspot.com/software/index.htm**

  A good description of the wedding planners and books for sale.

- **milestoneshops.com/1014/wedding/wedserv_1.html**

  Plan your entire wedding with this free software package.

- **www.rosemarycompany.com/wedding/wedserv_1.html**

- **www.frogwaresoftware.com**

  This one costs $129 after a 30 day free trial.

- **members.aol.com/WedSWare/owdgswr.html**

  A directory of wedding software.

- **www.fivestarsoftware.com/download.htm**

  Five star rating and $39 cost.

- **www.wedding-world.com/software.html**

  A national directory of wedding software services.

- **www.wedserve.com**

  Personal wedding sites, wedding software and answers to your questions.

You need, of course, only one planner so don't let the number of sites offering them intimidate you. Think of it as a reminder as to just how important having some sort of organization is.

Wedding Planning by State

Most of the crucial services for your wedding, such as sites and caterers and musicians, are only available locally. These sites show these services by State which will help you find local sources. Often you may find the listings are skimpy for your particular locale but this hopefully will improve as these sites mature.

www.wwwweddings.com

A comprehensive wedding directory broken down by State and including Europe and Canada.

usabride.com

Great State by State listings of local vendors as well as advice and everything else you'll need.

www.weddingvendors.com

A great site with loads of information and local vendors broken down by State and city.

www.bridal-links.com

Vendors listed by State.

Wedding Books

- **www.amazon.com**

  There are 982 titles available and the outlines on this splendid site are vastly better than I could do.

- **www.bn.com**

  Barnes and Noble lists 1,320 books when you type in "weddings" and thankfully they are arranged in order of popularity.

You really don't need old fashioned print books if you are comfortable using the internet for all your information and I dare say it's a lot cheaper than buying a pile of wedding books. But, if you are like me (old fashioned), you may feel more comfortable with one or two "processed trees" books that will be available even if the electricity fails. Your only problem will be in picking from the multitude available.

Theme Weddings

Some of these sites are for specific locations that won't be possible for your wedding but the ideas for different themes are valid. Mostly theme weddings involve renting costumes and then hoping the guests get in the swing of things and also dress appropriately.

- **www.vivalasvegasweddings.com**

  Gothic, Western, Victorian, Gangster, Egyptian etc.

- **www.hhs.se/eijs/anomaly/JWed.htm**

  Japanese wedding.

- **www.americancostumes.com**

  Costumes for theme weddings.

- **www.oldsacriverboat.com/**

  Riverboat weddings.

- **www.pbm.com/~lindahl/rialto/wed-trad-FAQ.text**

  Frequently asked questions about Medieval and renaissance theme weddings.

- **www.themeprops.com/bootsy/ttf/themepg.htm**

  Props for all kinds of wedding themes.

Wedding Web

- **www.weddingplan-it.com**

  Build your own free wedding web page. It's a great way to announce your wedding to the world.

- **waycoolweddings.com/home.htm**

  Links to other couples' wedding web pages which is a great way to get ideas for your wedding.

- **www.worldwidealbums.com**

  This company will help you prepare your own wedding web page.

- **www.pti69.com/weddings**

  Announce your wedding on the web and develop your personal wedding web page.

Some couples enjoy inviting all their friends (and the rest of the world for that matter) into all the planning of their wedding. By building your own web page you can share with others as much information as you like and post pictures after the event for all to see.

Marriage Law

Don't forget the marriage licenses and blood tests. These sites will give you the information you need.

- **www.ulc.net/laws.html**
  Marriage laws for each State.

- **www.fordham.edu/halsall/source/cjc-marriage.html**
  Ancient marriage laws.

- **www.legalinformation.net/infonet/family/common.html**
  Rules for common law marriages in the 11 States that allow them.

- **www.1040.com/comm.htm**
  Community property and common law.

- **marriage.about.com/home/marriage/library/weekly/aa052098.htm**
  Licenses and blood tests.

- www.divorcenet.com/il/il.html

  Answers common questions about marriage and divorce and all the laws in between.

- www.wam.umd.edu/~sek/wedding/abroad.html

  Legal requirements on marriage of U.S. citizens abroad.

- www.ulc.net/laws.html

  General marriage laws by State. This listing gives the same information as the one above but sites disappear and you do want your marriage to be legal, don't you?

You must apply for the marriage license together at the state agency and have proof of age and citizenship. The religious or civil official signs the marriage certificate after the wedding and sends it back to the proper agency. Overseas, marriage can be more complex though some tourist destinations encourage weddings and actually make it very simple.

- www.millersv.edu/~english/homepage/duncan/medfem/marriage.html

  An interesting essay on the laws and customs of marriage in the middle ages.

- marriage.about.com/home/marriage/library/weekly/aa052098.htm

  All the legal issues about getting married. Under General Marriage Laws there is an excellent State by State listing.

Gowns, Accessories and Attire

Gowns

Selecting the gown isn't the first thing you'll do to plan your wedding. Finding a site for the ceremony and reception are most critical and soon after you'll have to find a caterer and book musicians. But those are local tasks that are harder to do on the internet and since finding a gown probably is foremost on your mind, I'll start with that. You can do some initial screening of gowns on these sites and then make appointments with the local stores that carry the lines. Once you've selected a particular gown, you can, if you wish, check out the sites that offer to sell it to you on a discounted basis. You can also check the closeout and bargain stores. Finding the exact gown you want at a discount will take time but will save you big dollars.

Gowns can cost anywhere from a few hundred dollars to many thousands. As a general rule plan on spending 5% to 6% of your wedding budget on the gown.

www.ido.co.za/gowns.html

An excellent list of tips for selecting a gown style. If you want to appear taller, for example, choose a gown with a high neckline.

When shopping for the bridesmaids' gowns don't ever take along the whole party. You'll never get a consensus. Your maid of honor and your mother will be difficult enough.

- **www.mikawed.com/gsize_chart.html**
  Useful bridal gowns sizing chart.

- **www.bridalsearch.com**
  Can you believe, 15,000 gown images from 200 designers and available to search by designer, price, neckline or silhouette.

- **www.brides-r-us.com**
  Over 100 styles of gowns and matching accessories.

- **www.fivestarsoftware.com/weddinggown.htm**
  A good place to start with excellent tips for buying your wedding gown.

- **www.weddinguide.com/survival/gown.html**
  A nice one page introduction to selecting a gown.

Budget Gowns

- **www.gownsforless.com**
  Gowns that are trendy, flashy and young.
- **www.alt-gowns.com**
  Once worn gowns are half price.
- **www.gownsales.com**
  No frills bridal gowns and bridesmaid dresses.
- **www.uniquewedding.com**
  Consignment shop.
- **www.bridal-warehouse.com/front1.htm**
  Discount gowns.
- **www.cherishedweddinggowns.com/cgi-bin/cherished.cgi**
  Thousands of gowns on consignment, at steep discounts and well organized by designer, style and price. This site is also a place to retire your own gown.
- **www.bargainweddinggowns.com**
  Bargain gowns that are closeouts, samples and recycled. Find a $2,500 gown for under $300.

There are many, many sites that sell used, discontinued and surplus gowns at greatly reduced prices. You'll have to spend some time hunting but you will probably be rewarded with enormous savings.

Designer Gowns

Allow 3 to 6 months to select and fit your gown. Yes, you can do it in much less time but it will cost more for rush charges. If you are having it specially made you will probably have 3 fittings; a first one to correct errors and a final one shortly before the wedding to make sure everything is perfect. If you've decided to diet for your big day, don't select a size based on what you expect to be no matter how determined you are. Buy the gown for your present size. It's a lot easier to take a gown in than to let it out.

There are loads of great pictures of gowns in all the bridal magazines or you can view these sites for even more of a selection.

www.jimhjelmoccasions.com

Jim Hjelm's brides maid collection.

www.lazarobridal.com

Lazaro bridal gown collection and store locator.

www.amsale.com

Amsale Aberra's collection and retail locator.

www.alvinavalenta.com

The Alvina Valenta bridal gown collection and store locator.

www.bridalshowroom.com

A range of bridal designers and their catalogs.

www.mcbridals.com/

Mon Cheri Bridals actively discourages retailers from selling their gowns on the internet.

- **www.moonlightbridal.com**
  Moonlight Design's site with their catalog and store listing.

- **www.gowns.com**
  Sweetheart Gown's entire collection.

- **www.jasminebridal.com**
  Jasmine Haute Couture online catalog and store locator.

- **www.guzzobridal.com**
  The Guzzo collection site which proudly announces that their gowns start at $2,300.

- **www.alfredangelo.com/index1.htm**
  Welcome to the world of Alfred Angelo.

There are hundreds, probably tens of thousands of gown designers and I have listed only a few of them. This list does not indicate an endorsement. What do I know, I've been married for a hundred years. I'm sure many wonderful ones were omitted but this is just to give you an idea of the extraordinary choices available to you.

Your first trial with designer gowns is likely to be at a bridal salon. Most require appointments and it's a good idea to make one so you'll be given the royal treatment when you arrive. The lavish treatment is part of the program to make you feel very special. Don't let it prevent you from shopping carefully and wisely.

www.suzanne-ermann.com

Paris based wedding gown designer Suzanne Ermann's site. And it's all in French.

www.yumikatsura.com

Yumi Katsura's gowns and boutique information.

www.houseofbianchi.com

House of Bianchi showing custom designs from many designers.

www.billlevkoff.com

Bill Levkoff's site with gowns designed by Veronica Cifone.

www.berte.com

Janell Berte's site.

www.marisabridals.com

This site has the designs by Tamara Kristen.

- **www.moniquebridal.com**
  Monique Luo couturre.

- **www.saisonblanche.com**
  Saison Blanche designs.

- **www.pronovias.com**
  With offices throughout Europe, Pronovias seems especially exclusive.

- **www.waters.com**
  The site of Watters and Watters.

- **www.stpucchi.com/Main.htm**
  The St. Pucchi collection.

- **www.willowsandivy.com**
  Willows and Ivy gowns.

When looking for a bridal shop check with former customers. Establish the cost of alterations in advance and find out exactly when the shop will be ordering your dress. Get everything down in writing especially the delivery date.

Sites that Claim to Discount Designer Gowns

If you are willing to spend the time you will be able to find someone willing to sell you most any designer gown at a discount. While you will be saving a significant amount of money, recognize that you may miss out on being treated like a princess by a full service bridal boutique where all the sales people will be showering you with lavish attention. It's a pretty nice feeling.

- **www.netbride.com**
  Discounted gowns.

- **www.bridalpenthouse.com**
  A selection of designer gowns at discount prices.

- **www.stylebridal.com**
  This large California store always has over 300 gowns priced from $99 to $299.

- **www.bridalmarketplace.com**
  Provide The Bridal Market Place with the gown manufacturer and style number and they claim to discount it up to 50%.

- **www.savvybridal.com**
  Discounts of 20% to 40% on nationally advertised gowns.

- **www.bridalsonline.com**
  Explains how to order gowns online from the best designers at 20% to 40% discounts.

- **www.davidsbridal.com**
  A chain of over 100 retail stores with a 132 page catalog you can order.

- **www.dreamweavers.com/gowns/index.cfm**
  Almost 1,000 gowns to view with the ability to search by designer, price, fabric, style etc.

- **www.abridesbestfriend.com/dresses.htm**
  Links to almost 50 gown manufacturers and their catalogs and excellent dress suggestions for different levels of formality.

- **www.bridalpenthouse.com**
  Ontario based bridal boutique offers choices by designer.

- **www.dessy.com**
  An impressive site that shows the whole Dessy line in all available colors with lots of swatch books you can send for and where to find retailers.

Keep an open mind when shopping for a gown. You may have your heart set on one style but keep looking in the mirrors and you will be surprised how many options present themselves. The one or two advisors you take along can be a big help here.

Large Size Gowns and Lingerie

So many companies specialize in large size gowns that there is no difficulty fitting brides or brides' attendants elegantly.

- **www.faqs.org/faqs/fat-acceptance-faq/clothing/us**
  Loads of information on where to find wedding gowns in large sizes. Frequently asked questions about clothing for big folks.

- **lingerieatlarge.com**
  Sexy lingerie in large sizes.

- **www.silverliningplus.com/bio.html**
  Wedding gowns and lingerie in sizes 14 to 26.

- **www.todaysbride.ca/products/fashion.html**
  A list of Canadian Bridal shops, one of which, Big, Bold and Beautiful specializes in sizes 14 to 30.

- **www.largeworld.com/fashion.html**
  Lists almost a hundred manufactures, stores and designers that specialize in clothing for large women. Here is the place to find that swim suit for your honeymoon.

- **www.cyberinfo.com/large.htm**
  This directory of Resources for Large Women costs $4.95.

- **www.dimensionsmagazine.com/fashion/page2.shtml**
  An excellent list of places to buy gowns in large sizes.

Vintage Wedding Gowns

If grandma's wedding dress just doesn't suit you and your heart is set on a period wedding there are lots of sites with gowns dating back to the early 1800's. You can find real bargains in antique and used gowns but make sure you have a good seamstress lined up to alter it.

- **www.victorianelegance.com**
  Vintage and antique wedding gowns and clothing from 1800 on.

- **www.vintagewedding.com**
  Vintage wedding attire for the entire bridal party.

- **www.ashlandvintage.com/wedding.html**
  A small collection of vintage gowns.

- **www.usedweddingdresses.com/**
  A large collection of antique and used dresses listed by category.

- **home.att.net/~design-house**
  This site has over 250 antique and vintage wedding gowns.

- **hometown.aol.com/gowns4you/index.html**
  Vintage gowns from the Victorian, Swing eras as well as the 50's, 60's, and 70's.

When buying an antique or used gown inspect it carefully for stains, tears or other defects. Again be sure to have a seamstress. Bridal shops will not alter a gown bought elsewhere.

www.neens.com

Antique and vintage clothing.

www.yosa.com/catalog/wedding.html

Drawings and photos of antique wedding dresses that can be made for your wedding.

www.tias.com/stores/vr/gowns-1.html

Vintage wedding gowns, many of which are quite inexpensive.

home.att.net/~design-house

Gulden & Brown's site with over 200 vintage styles and prices.

www.fairyfashion.de/index.html

Designer made medieval to renaissance wedding gowns and bridesmaid gowns.

www.411web.com/A/ALADIESGALLERYOFFINEANTIQUES/product.htm

Antique lace and textiles as well as wedding gowns.

Cleaning, Storing and Restoring Wedding Gowns

www.agesahead.com
Cleaning and restoring antique wedding gowns.

consumersgo.to/barkersfinedrycleaning/pagell.html
Wedding gown preservation.

www.bruhnsbridal.com
You can wear grandma's gown even if it's yellowed because these folks can restore its original color.

www.gownmedic.com/pres.htm
Specialists in heirloom preservation.

www.gownpreserve.com/warranty.htm
Gown preservation with a written guarantee.

users.ap.net/~finnyboy/wgown.htm
Acid free packaging insures generations of wearability.

www.arrow-care.com
Nationwide bridal gown cleaning and preserving services.

While the sites listed claim to specialize in gown preservation I suspect any good cleaner can do the job.

Bridal Headpieces and Veils

There are lots of choices for headpieces and veils from custom designs to economy $69 pieces. This is an easy item to order online; just be sure it complements the style of your dress.

starlightbridals.com

This small company specializes in bridal headpieces and veils for reasonable prices.

www.annabridal.com

Lots of headpieces.

bettywales.com

Hats, tiaras and veils.

www.bridalheadpieces.com/laurind.htm

A specialist in creating and restoring headpieces and veils.

www.ansoniabridal.com/home.htm

Their catalog shows 300 different designs of veils and tiaras.

www.mikawed.com

On-line sales of bridal veils, hats, gloves as well as gowns.

www.ansoniabridal.com/home.htm
Milliner's Supply Co. has been selling bridal veils, gloves and hats since 1911.

www.bridalcreations.com
Photos and descriptions of veils and tiaras.

www.hobi-tulle.com
A catalog of veils and tulle bands.

giselle.keybuys.com
Over 100 headpieces and veils as well as custom designs.

www.bridalstuff.com
Bridal veils and headpieces for $69.

www.galaxymall.com/fashion/wedding
Bridal headpieces and custom veiling.

www.designonevab.com
Bridal hats and veils plus Roaring 20's wedding caps and other items for theme weddings.

www.romanticheadlines.com/index.htm
Large collection of veils, tiaras, hats and accessories.

www.belaireveils.com
Bel Aire bridal veils.

www.hatshatshats.com
Custom designed, handblocked hats and veils.

www.nque.com/~veils
Bridal veil manufacturer.

You should allow 2 months for ordering your headpiece and it's a good idea to get it early so you have time for a few trial runs with your hairdresser.

Wedding Shoes

Shoes are something that it's a good idea to try on before you buy but if you're sure of your size and can return it you can try buying them online.

- **www.nycshoes.com/exclusives/sneaker.htm**
  A wedding sneaker for $39. Sounds like a pretty comfy shoe, especially during the reception.
- **www.e-weddingshoes.com**
  Wedding shoes listed by heel height.
- **www.nycshoes.com/appliques/44664.htm**
  NYC shoes and accessories.
- **www.bellinghams.demon.co.uk/shoes2.htm**
  Silk and satin shoes from England.
- **www.thoseshoes.com/custom.html**
  Custom wedding shoes that look pretty wild.
- **www.theglassslipper.com/laceclr.htm**
  Lace and clear shoes.
- **www.bridalshoes.com**
  A wide selection of bridal shoes.
- **www.nque.com/~veils**
  Dyeable shoes and handbags.

Intimates

- **www.imt.net/~lingerie/index.html**
  Custom tailored intimates.
- **www.lingerie-store.com**
  The descriptions are in French as well as English so it must be sexy.
- **www.lingeriemart.com**
  They claim to be the largest source for all kinds of wholesale lingerie and from the size of their site I can believe it.
- **www.shoptheplaza.com/playstor/4ever.html**
  A large selection of sexy and erotic lingerie.
- **www.lusciouswear.com**
  Very sexy fine lingerie.
- **emporium.net/avalon**
  "Drift to a place where romance and innocence meet."
- **www.ascantylingerie.com/bridal.htm**
  Extensive bridal collection.
- **www.business.mcmaster.ca/courses/s727/davio/bridal.htm**
  Bridal peignoir sets, lace chiffon charmeuse gowns, baby doll sets and such.
- **www.internetbridalmarket.com/q-t.htm**
  Bridal lingerie and intimates.

> You could let your groom help you pick out the intimates for your wedding night and honeymoon and he'd probably love it but then you wouldn't be able to surprise him.

You really don't need this many sites for selecting intimates but you must admit they are fun. Some of them have intimates so sexy and exciting that you'll have to keep them carefully hidden from the groom or he'll never be able to wait for the wedding night.

www.azzuma.com

Pamper yourself in luxurious French lingerie.

www.fredericks.com

Frederick's of Hollywood site.

www.victoriassecret.com/index.html

The Victoria's Secret site is magnificently well done and the quality of the intimates impeccable.

www.oohlala-kirkland.com

Catalog of bustiers, body suits, camisoles, sleepwear, teddies, chemises and more, in regular and plus sizes.

www.firoza.com/peignoirs.html

A classy collection of designer peignoirs and intimate apparel.

www.silknchoices.com

Silk and lace bras, panties and everything else.

Spas

www.spatime.com

Great spas of the world to help make the bride even more beautiful They must work because they cost $550 to $1,500 and that's without the airfare to some of the exotic locations like France, Hungary and Thailand.

www.mandalaybay.com/spa.html

Located in Las Vegas the Spa Mandalay offers everything from volcanic dust treatment to beautiful back facials (whatever that is).

www.spafinders.com

Features a spa search for locations around the world, as well as online gift certificates, magazine subscription, healthy cuisine ideas, and discounted specials.

If you feel the need for a little toning before your wedding here is a list of some spas that will beat you into shape in no time at all. Spas make wonderful locations for bachelorette parties and showers as well. You can splurge with a week long program that will make a new you or just visit for a few hours and feel sparkling refurbished.

The goal of many of the really good spas is to introduce and educate you in the ways of a healthy life style rather than just to primp you up for the short term. This includes lots of classes in diet, food preparation and exercise.

- **women.com/travel/spas**
  Reviews and readers polls of the world's top spa's.

- **www.worldhealthspa.com/index.htm**
  A world health spa directory with over 500 listings.

- **www.canyonranch.com**
  The home site of the famous Canyon Ranch Spa in Lenox MA and Tucson AZ.

- **spas.about.com/travel/spas/library/weekly/aa112199.htm**
  The world's top spas from Conde Nast's 1999 readers choice.

- **spas.about.com/travel/spas/msub9sw.htm**
  Spa resorts in Switzerland.

- **spas.about.com/travel/spas/**
  More than you will ever want to know about spas including lists of spas and descriptions of every treatment.

- **spas.about.com/travel/spas/msub7.htm**
  This link of spa travel agents will help you pick out a perfect spa and get you there.

Wedding Horoscopes

In many cultures getting married on an auspicious day is absolutely critical. In the event you believe in this nonsense here are a list of sites that can give you some information.

- **www.directoryindia.com/wedding**

  Wedding astrology services. Why get married on an inauspicious day? These astrologers seem to be mainly in India so they should know.

- **tncweddings.women.com/tc/horoscop**

  Town and Country wedding horoscopes. Find out if you are right for each other.

- **www.dailystars.com**

  A free daily horoscope.

- **www.usbridalguide.com/special/horoscope.htm**

  US Bridal wedding horoscopes.

- **weddingdreams.net/horoscope.html**

  More daily horoscope readings. I certainly hope all these different ones agree.

- **wedding.gogrrl.com/link/4_superstition.asp**

  Wedding superstitions and gossip.

- **women.astrology.com/juno/**

  Investigate to see if your match was really made in heaven.

- **www.vangelis.com.au/default.htm**

  The astrological charts cost $9.95 to $14.95 but the wedding superstitions are free and they are charming.

Wedding Jewelry

I hope you have your engagement ring by now since the internet doesn't seem like a very romantic way to get that piece of jewelry. It is, however, a good way to investigate wedding bands and jewelry gifts for the wedding party.

- **www.diamondspecialists.com/home.htm**

  You can buy your diamond on-line after attending a free 15 minute diamond seminar.

- **www.tradersofbabylon.com**

  Specialist in wedding bands and engagement rings.

- **www.jewelersinternet.com**

  With 50,000 products on this site you should be able to find something you like.

- **www.christianbauer.com**

  European designed wedding bands and rings.

- **www.ajewelrymall.com**

  An extensive source of jewelry sorted by price, stores and function.

www.mokume-gane.com

Mokume gane japanese method jewelry for rings and wedding objects.

www.shahasp.com

Handmade bridal jewelry.

3djeweler.com

Custom jewelry designer.

www.bridal-jewelry.com

Their selection of bridal jewelry goes to the thousands.

www.adiamondisforever.com/M/index.htm

De Beers diamond company gives excellent advice on buying a diamond.

www.quantumweb.com/daoud/design.html

Very interesting Celtic and other exotic wedding band designs.

ejeweler.com/majors.htm

An extensive line of wedding bands from different manufacturers.

Choose your jeweler with care from recommendations and Better Business Bureau lists and remember that diamonds and gold don't really sell at 40% to 60% off.

Tuxedos

Since guys are always confused with the different designations of formal wear here is a breakdown of which is what.

Contemporary Weddings

Very formal evening	Tailcoat
Semi Formal evening	Tuxedo or Tailcoat
Very Formal day	Cutaway-gray with striped trousers
Formal day	Tailcoat

Traditional Weddings

Very formal evening	Tailcoat
Formal evening	Tuxedo or white dinner jacket in summer
Very formal day	Cutaway coat, gray
Semi formal day	Gray stroller with striped trousers

www.tuxonthenet.com

This site answers those perennial questions about tying the bow tie, which way the pleats in the cummerbund face and tux styles along with information on their 70 stores.

www.jimsfw.com

Tuxedo suggestions for different kinds of weddings.

www.formalwear.org

International Formalwear Association site with good guides to tuxedos and stores.

- **www.gingiss.com**

  Formalwear manufacturer with lists of retail stores.

- **www.selix.com/weddings.htm**

  Wedding packages of formalwear.

- **www.tuxonthenet.com/rental**

  Rental chain with a good guide.

- **www.california-bride.com/wtformal.html**

  Formalwear styles. They begin by saying "There are no hard and fast rules."

- **www.abridesdream.com/tuxedos.html**

  $54 to $90 per tuxedo.

- **tuxedos4u.com/home.htm**

  A complete guide to men's formalwear along with a store guide.

These sites are mostly retail tuxedo sites but you'll get some ideas from them as to styles and prices.

Wedding Photography

After examining samples of a photographer's work make sure you feel a rapport with them so they will understand what kind of photographs you want. Most importantly, make sure the photographer isn't the kind who takes over your wedding.

- **www.weddingbureau.com**

  The Wedding Bureau claims to be a listing of some of the nation's best photojournalists who are available to photograph your wedding. Most major cities are covered.

- **www.ekfoto.com/question.htm**

  Answers to the most frequently asked questions about wedding photography.

- **amateurphoto.about.com/library/weekly/aa042698.htm**

  This is an article about photographer etiquette and the ceremony. I liked the opening line that "being a good wedding photographer is remembering the wedding is not for you." This is worth reading before you hire the photographer.

- **www.worth.net/photos/info1.html**

  If you want to be really knowledgeable about wedding photography read this before talking to your photography candidates. It's great information.

Single Use Wedding Cameras

- www.candideventcameras.com
- www.party411.com/gifts-200.html
- www.theweddinglab.com
- www.westons.com/solocam.htm
- www.cngdisposablecamera.com
- www.wedmart.com/camera

Why settle for one photographer when you can have all your guests catch special moments. Disposable cameras are inexpensive and really extend the coverage of your reception. Here are some sites that sell them. Shop around. You can find cameras for around $6 if you look.

Videography

The goal of a great wedding video is to have it so interesting that you would watch it even without knowing the participants. To have a memorable video you need an individual who is sensitive to the event. You want a videographer who will do close ups and intimates and not just blast away with a wide angle lens. Be sure to check with the religious officials to find out if they allow videotaping of the ceremony. Also coordinate between the videographer and photographer to make sure they will cooperate. Nothing is worse than the two of them fighting.

www.videocrafters.com/html/guide.htm

A great guide to wedding videography by a studio in the Virginia-Maryland-DC area.

www.wco.com/~wedtips/wttipvi.html

A short description of what to look for and ask when choosing a wedding videographer.

www.videouniversity.com

If you are going to video the wedding yourself get some tips from Video University first.

www.weddingmagazine.net

The Wedding Magazine will deliver 2 professional crews to film your wedding anywhere in the country.

www.byreconly.com/featvide.htm

Brief recommendations on choosing the right videographer.

www.lindelle.com

Lindelle is a large firm covering the mid Atlantic states.

www.hecks.net/Wedding_Videography/wedding_videography.html

A professional wedding videography firm covering the mid Atlantic states.

Uncle Harry can probably make a passable video of your wedding. His difficulty will be in finding a camera that will provide adequate quality in very poor light. Professional equipment is usually needed and these are expensive. Unless he has experience editing, the video will be dull and too long.

Wedding Invitations

It would seem that any printer could produce your invitations but the industry has become dominated by a few large firms who turn out magnificent catalogs showing an enormous range of styles. These catalogs make it easy to pick out papers, colors, type, borders, and ornamentation and are usually more economical than creating the designs yourself from scratch. Any stationery store and many printers have these catalogs or you can order direct from this on-line list.

While most of your friends will already know of the date and place, your invitation is the first formal impression the guests will have of your wedding. Make certain the invitation choice reflects your style and taste.

- www.invitationsbydawn.com
- www.theamericanwedding.com
- www.wedding.orders.com
- www.rexcraft.com
- www.invitationstores.org
- www.ourbegining.com

- www.princessweddings.com
- www.pinktulip.org
- www.graficacquaviva.it
- www.ourbeginning.com/obhome.nsf
- www.discount-invitation.com
- www.botanicalpaperworks.mb.ca/index.html
- www.birchcraft.com/etiquett.htm
  This site answers some stationery etiquette questions.
- www.abbey-print.freeserve.co.uk
- home.ica.net/~sfleming/greenen.htm

The first thing everyone does when receiving an invitation is to run their fingers over the printing to see if it is engraved. Real engraved printing requires making a mold to stamp the paper. The ink fills in the indentation and you can feel the bumps. To tell if something is engraved you look on the back for a wrinkled appearance under the letters.

Thermography is a much cheaper way of achieving a feel similar to engraving and almost everyone uses it these days.

Software for Printing Invitations

You can save most of the cost of invitations and other announcements by printing them yourself on your computer. Here are some sites that offer programs to do this.

- www.ed-it.com/wedding
- www.ed-it.com/p_wedsoc.htm
- www.artworksuk.com
- www.geocities.com/SouthBeach/Terrace/4135
- www.invitationsetc.com

Wedding Calligraphy

- **members.aol.com/istommoin**
  Artistic calligraphy with a 3 week lead time.

- **www.bridesmate.com**
  If you order your invitations from this company they offer free calligraphy addressing.

- **www.calligraphyservices.com**
  A lovely calligraphy service for weddings.

- **www.bcreativecalligraphy.com**
  Creative calligraphy for weddings.

- **members.aol.com/kshader/zoom7**
  Wedding vows in hand lettered calligraphy.

- **www.webparlor.com/cottage**
  Hand lettered calligraphy and watercolors.

- **www.prewedding.com**
  They give prices for all your wedding printing and calligraphy needs.

If your handwriting is beautiful, there is a certain elegance in addressing your invitations personally. Hand calligraphy is available to take over the job from those of us whose handwriting is "chicken scratches" and nowadays there are even computer fonts that imitate fine caligraphy.

Wedding Music

Your choice of music is obviously a very personal matter and you probably have some very special tastes that you'll want to incorporate into your wedding. The following sites will give you some very extensive music ideas for the ceremony and reception.

- **www.weddingmusic2dance.com**
  Wedding dance music.

- **www.weddingmusic.co.uk**
  Wedding music CDs.

- **hometown.aol.com/weddingmus/myhomepage/index.html**
  A wedding music guide for $11.95.

- **www.lib.virginia.edu/MusicLib/collect/wedding.html**
  A collection of classical wedding music.

- **www.homestead.com/weddingoriginals/wedding_music_originals.html**
  Custom music for your wedding.

www.weddingusa.com/plan/angel.htm
A guide to choosing music.

www.findyourdj.com
Find your DJ with this listing of professionals.

www.partypros.com
Lists of ceremony and reception music plus tips on finding a professional DJ.

www.thesaxman.com
This organization composes original music and jingles for your wedding.

www.wedday.com/entertainment
A guide for selecting wedding music.

weddingwire.com/songs.htm
An exhaustive file of wedding reception songs.

A choir director or organist at your ceremony site is an excellent source for music suggestions. The music can reflect joy or solemnity or whatever emotions you feel are most appropriate.

You can interview bands and DJ's by going to affairs where they are working. Don't be afraid to dance or taste the hors d'oeuvres; it's great fun and you'll get some ideas for your own wedding.

Music can make or break your reception. Insist on a written contract and read it to find out how long they'll play and how many breaks they'll take. Also talk to them about the volume of their music which often drives the older guests batty.

members.tripod.co.uk/phillip_sear/choosing1.html

Piano music for civil weddings.

www.radiopro.com/wedding_planning/wedding_dj.htm

Good advice on selecting a wedding DJ.

www.abridesbestfriend.com/music.htm

Original music suggestions for each part of your wedding.

www.weddingglobe.com/songs.asp

Wedding song library with suggestions for each wedding event.

www.weddingguide.co.uk/HymnsRorYourService.html

A guide to hymns for your service.

Live Butterflies

- www.butterflycelebration.com
- www.butterflyinmiami.com
- www.floridamonarch.com
- members.tripod.com/~WingsBeauty
- www.butterflyreleases.com/zhbut~4.htm
- mgfx.com/butterflywedding
- www.themonarchy.com
- www.butterflyblessings.com
- butterflies.hypermart.net/releases.html
- www.magicalmonarchs.com/release.htm
- www.butterflyrelease.com/release.html
- users.penn.com/%7Efragacre/photo%7E1.htm

Butterfly releases are a lovely touch for weddings. Releasing butterflies at the end of the ceremony will have all your guests gasping and is an exciting alternative to throwing rice. In case you don't have hundreds in your backyard here are a few places that sell them. Be sure to follow instructions for keeping the butterflies alive and be particularly careful on very hot or cold days.

Dove Releases

If you are looking for a conclusion to your ceremony even more dramatic than a butterfly release, a flock of snow white love birds rising from the ground is the way to go. It sounds expensive but actually you just rent them and hopefully most return to their cages. It's a regional kind of operation but here are a few sites so you can get an idea of how they operate.

- www.doverelease.com
- www.weddinglinks.com/mem/Doves.htm
- lovedoves.com/home.html
- www.weddingdetails.com/dove
- www.whitebird.com/Weddings.htm

Wedding Flowers

- **www.aristonflorist.com/wedding.html**
  Wedding flower check list.

- **www.bridesandgrooms.com/weddings/flowers.html**
  Wedding flowers and arrangements.

- **www.wedplan.com/flwrsart.htm**
  Wedding planning articles and frequently asked questions about flowers.

- **www.stretcher.com/stories/970505b.cfm**
  Frugal wedding flowers and tips on how to keep costs down.

- **www.weddingcircle.com/fyi/floral.htm**
  Suggestions on creating your own wedding floral arrangements.

These sites give lots of suggestions for your wedding flower arrangements as well as tips on doing it yourself and contacts for florists in your area. Weddings are a labor intensive event and if you're getting married near Valentines or Mothers Day or around a holiday line up a florist at least 3 months in advance.

Word of mouth is a good starting point for finding a local florist as is attending wedding expos. Ask to see photos of other weddings they have done and check their references.

www.fleurspermail.com

Silk wedding flowers.

www.buyflowers.net

This site puts you in touch with florists in your area to meet your budget.

gbwg.com/wedding_flowers.html

Strategies for you to orchestrate perfect floral arrangements.

www.weddingcircle.com/services/florists.htm

Florist links.

webhome.idirect.com/~sdfloral/

Claims low prices on flowers for weddings nationwide.

Preserving Wedding Flowers

- **home.earthlink.net/~julie_ca**
  Preserve your wedding flowers forever.

- **www.weddingdetails.com/leamans**
  Freeze dried bouquets and shadow boxes.

- **www.pressedflowers.com**
  Flowers pressed to preserve them forever.

- **www.syrweddings.com/vincenza**
  Wedding flower preserving.

- **www.mallwest.com/katesfdf**
  Freeze dried preservation of your wedding bouquet.

- **www.4everafter.com**
  Preserving your bridal bouquet.

- **www.pressedflowers.co.uk**
  Pressing your flowers with an expert English company.

After spending all that money on your bouquet you will likely want to preserve it forever. The preservation may cost more than the bouquet itself so ask yourself if relatively inexpensive pressing or drying would be more practical.

Wedding Accessories

This is a broad category that includes so many little items such as guest books, favors, napkins, garters, wedding rice, photo albums, wedding party gifts, cake accessories, candles, ring bearer pillows, vehicle kits and so many more things you'll wonder if there is time left to actually get married.

- **www.lillianrose.com**
  Bells and bubbles and bows and books among other things.

- **www.hazels.com**
  Western wedding accessories.

- **www.weddinghelpers.com/romanc.html**
  Marriage certificates, traditional, elegant and humorous along with name change kits and other stuff.

- **www.americanbridal.com**
  Ring bearer pillows, cake knives, guest books and lots of other stuff you didn't know you need.

- **www.elegantacc.com**
  Original, elegant accessories.

- **www.mgcpuzzles.com/mgcpuzzles/occasions/weddings.html**
  Custom made wood favors or gift jigsaw puzzles.

- **www.wedguide.com**
  The wedding store at this site has a host of gifts and accessories.

- **www.accentbridal.com**
  Gloves as well as other accessories.

- **members.aol.com/tndrhart2/favor.html**
  Wedding accessories.
- **www.bridalink.com/store2**
  Accessories. Favors and ornaments.
- **www3.ns.sympatico.ca/tilly/wedhome.html**
  Cake tops, unity sets, angels, ring pillows and stuff.
- **pw1.netcom.com/~mymia/partyangel.html**
  Wedding favors in crystal, marble and porcelain.
- **mmcreations.com/wedding**
  Wedding favors and accessories.
- **www.weddingpackage.com**
  Gifts and accessories and supplies to make your own.
- **www.favorite-things.com/Supply_Index.htm**
  Pages of favors, accessories and supplies.
- **www.jtdesigns.com**
  Traditional design favors and accessories.

If you are so inclined, the wedding accessories are a perfect area to exercise your creative and craft talents. Check the Wedding Craft page for ideas and supplies.

Cake Tops

Wedding cakes in general can be much more expensive than you can imagine. Don't leave arranging for one for the last minute. So much work is involved that some bakers only take on one a week. While the caterer or baker may take care of your cake top, if you want something special like figures representing the two of you, these sites will give you some idea of what's available.

- **www.cakeemporium.com/graphics/ornpm2.htm**
  Doll cake tops.
- **www.katinc.com/~horvath/caketops.htm**
  Handblown glass cake tops.
- **www.katinc.com/%7Ehorvath/**
  Handblown glass cake tops.
- **www.dollonline.com/wedding.htm**
  Doll cake tops.
- **www.wwweddings.com/National/cakes.htm**
  Custom wedding cake tops.
- **www.cybercakes.com/wedding_toppers.html**
  Cake tops.
- **www.miscaketops.com**
  Personalized cake tops made to look like you.
- **www.caketop.com**
  Hand blown cake tops.
- **www.americancakesupply.com**
  Cake decorating supplies.

Wedding Favors

Whether you are looking for imaginative or inexpensive (and they are not mutually exclusive) favors to give to your wedding party and guests these sites will give you some ideas of what is available.

- **www.receptionfavors.com**

  A broad line of wedding favors from fortune cookies to porcelain.

- **www.receptionfavors.com**

  Wedding favors plus links to loads of very good wedding sites.

- **www.lymans.com/akiss**

  Original glass sculptures for favors and cake tops.

- **www.adreamwedding.com**

  Favors and miscellaneous items along with chat and advice and other information.

- **www.expressionsgifts.com**

  Personalized favors such as seeds, note pads and sachets.

- **www.weddingfavors.com**

  Boxes, bubbles, bells, chocolate and almonds.

Personalized Favors

Wedding favors are a very broad category and you might try to focus your choices by giving gifts that tie into the bride's and groom's particular interests or life style. Nature lovers could give seeds or plants; wine connoisseurs, bottles with personalized labels etc.

- **www.lymans.com/akiss**
  Glass sculptures with hand engraved sayings.
- **www.photowrappers.com**
  Favors consisting of a custom photograph candy bar wrapper.
- **www.favorsbyserendipity.com**
  A wide selection of favors on a well illustrated site.
- **www.fotolabels.com**
  You put this company's personalized, photographic labels on bottles of wine or champagne at your wedding.
- **forapuzzle.com/4/wedding_favors.htm**
  Custom made wooden jigsaw puzzle favors with your photograph or message.
- **www.wholesalefavors.com/wedding.htm**
  A list and photos of bells, boxes, and frame favors.
- **www.cdcelebrations.com**
  Custom CD's for wedding favors.

Chocolate Favors

- www.chocolatecheers.com
- www.heresheis.com
- www.moosiewrapper.com
- www.tomandsallys.com
- www.1chocolaterose.com/wedding.htm
- www.cherubsandchocolate.com/Price_List.htm
- www.cwpd.com/vse/tulle.html

Everyone loves a chocolate favor or dessert and some of the ones listed here will destroy your diet when you sample them. Check carefully with the supplier if you are shipping them in warm weather.

Wedding Crafts

There are many wedding items you can make yourself and have the satisfaction of creating the items or favors as well as saving lots of money.

weddings.about.com/style/weddings/msubmenu01.htm

Great information about wedding crafts from About.com.

www.craftmall.com/forums/wedding/index1.html

Exchange ideas about wedding crafts on this site.

www.ultimatewedding.com/favors

Dozens of ideas for creating favors in six categories, from candies to bells to sport themes.

wedcraft.com

A very extensive compilation of wedding craft ideas and sources.

www.favorite-things.com/Supply_Index.htm

A supply source of materials you may need for your wedding crafts.

www.wednet.com/inspire/favors.asp

Very sound ideas and tips on wedding favors.

Registering for Gifts

If you register for pink crystal or Limoge china, that is likely what you will receive for gifts. But you don't have to listen to your mother. You can register for neat camping equipment at REI or LL Bean, or electronic equipment or tandem bikes, ski stuff or golf clubs. Be creative and establish your priorities early in your engagement. Registering for nothing may give people the hint that you prefer cash.

Places To Register Online

There are endless stores with which to register and I have listed a few of the most popular. Most allow online registration but some require store or phone contact.

Since your friends and family are going to give you gifts it's simple common sense to let them give you gifts you actually want. So you'll register with these stores that are absolutely thrilled to be getting all this additional business. While this is all very logical and economically sound, for some reason it isn't considered polite to tell people where you are registered unless they ask and you can't tell them exactly what you want. One way around this is to have the people who are coordinating your "surprise" engagement shower include a list of places you are registered on the invitation. Then you have to hope you get things you really want, because you can't complain if you are disappointed.

Each gift requires a thank you note, naturally, and you'll be smart to write them as each gift comes in rather than wait till you're back from the honeymoon. Not only will there be fewer mix ups but the overwhelming size of the task won't be hanging over you.

You can also register with many travel agencies to have your guests help with the honeymoon.

Places to Register

- **www.bedbathandbeyond.com**

  Bed Bath & Beyond offers online registry plus nationwide stores.

- **www.crateandbarrel.com**

  In the future registrants will be able to register and edit online with Crate and Barrel.

- **www.bloomingdales.com**

  The registry at Bloomingdales is nationwide.

- **www.williamssonomainc.com**

  Lots of high-end kitchen accessories. This is also the site for Pottery Barn with affordable furniture and accessories.

- **www.ross-simons.com/registry**

  Ross-Simons' bridal registry for china, crystal, tableware and home furnishings.

- **www.dillards.com/registry/index.html**

  Dillards, with 300 stores nationwide, has an easy-to-use wedding registry for gifts and accessories.

Make sure the stores you register at are accessible to the majority of your guests. Most large chains with hundreds of stores are convenient for everyone. If your guests know how, generally, to order online it makes your choices much easier.

Places To Register

When registering, try to achieve some balance in your list between formal dinnerware and everyday things and even big ticket items. Some guests may prefer something that you'll use every day and some may want to get together with others to buy something major.

- **www.fortunoff.com**

  Fortunoff has over 20,000 in stock items.

- **www.jcpenny.com**

  You can't register online but there are 1,000 stores.

- **www.williams-sonoma.com**

  Williams-Sonoma knows that some of the best relationships start in the kitchen.

- **www.pier1.com**

  You can't yet register online but this is a favorite bridal registration spot.

- **www.weddingchannel.com**

  Their Gift Registry Alliance allows you to register at Macy's, The Bon Marché, Burdines, Goldsmith's, Lazarus, Rich's and Stern's.

- **www.macysbridal.com**

  Macy's well designed registry site.

- **www.potterybarn.com**

  Affordable and casual furniture and accessories at Pottery Barn.

Registering for Sporting Goods and Electronics

- **www.rei.com**

  Recreational Equipment Co. site with extensive outdoor and camping items and they even have a gift registry.

- **www.llbean.com**

  The famous L.L. Bean store with an extensive line of outdoor equipment and clothing.

- **www.backcountrygear.com/gift/wishlist_main.cfm**

  Register for all sorts of camping gear.

- **www.altrec.com/shop/dir/9**

  A great site for outdoor gear but unfortunately not yet set up for gift registry.

Registries for sporting goods, electronic items, artwork or furniture are also becoming more popular along with the traditional china, silver and glass options. Best Buy will have a bridal registry by 2001 but for now your best bet is to register for appliances and electronics at a department store.

China and Dinnerware

It's not hard to find sources of china and dinnerware but perhaps this listing of manufacturers will save you a few minutes by listing places you can view some styles.

www.lenox.com

Expert advice and all the details about Lenox.

www.noritakechina.com

You can view the whole Noritake line here.

www.mikasa.com

All of Mikasa with online shopping or store directory.

www.waterford-usa.com

Waterford crystal and china.

www.royal-doulton.com

A lovely site with all the Royal Doulton products.

www.spode.co.uk

Classic china from this 200 year old company.

China and Dinnerware

- **www.wedgwood.co.uk**

  The famous Wedgwood line.

- **www.dansk.com**

  Lots more than china available from Dansk.

- **www.pfaltzgraff.com**

  Lots of patterns from Pfaltzgraff even if you can't spell the name.

- **www.sango.com**

  Stoneware, porcelain and fine china from Indonesia.

- **www.royal-tara.com**

  Royal Tara China from Ireland.

Fine dinnerware may not seem the gift with the highest priority when you first get married and need so many other necessities, but the truth is if you don't get it now it's unlikely you ever will. The same is true for silverware and crystal.

Linens

Most couples probably already have a supply of towels and bed things but registering for gifts gives you an opportunity to pull everything together into a cohesive style.

- **www.linensnthings.com**

  Linens and Things specializes in name brands and has online registration plus over 230 stores.

- **www.lnthings.com/bridal.html**

  Bridal registry site of Linens and Things.

- **www.bedbathandbeyond.com**

  Bed Bath and Beyond online store and bridal registry.

- **www.bloomingdales.com**

  Bloomingdale's has lots more than linens to register for.

- **www.visatablelinen.com/store.html**

  Miliken's site with good linen information like napkin folding and table size guides.

- **www.domenicarosa.com**

  Domenica Rosa's fine imported linens and silks.

- **www.superexpo.com/HF-linens.htm**

  A super expo of several dozen linen sources.

Crystal and Stemware

- **www.orrefors.com**
  Orrefors catalog in English or Swedish.

- **www.lenox.com**
  Lenox has an extensive line of crystal as well as china.

- **www.waterford-usa.com**
  Waterford also has an extensive line of crystal.

- **www.riedelcrystal.com/index.htm**
  Riedel specializes in stemware for wine and you won't believe the selection of glasses for different drinks.

- **www.kristallwelten.com**
  The Swarovski line shown in a site that will blow your mind.

- **www.mikasa.com**
  Mikasa's line of stemware.

- **www.ywh.com/manufacturer/stemware/Atlantis/Atlantis-list.html**
  Atlantis crystal cut by Cristal of Portugal.

There are loads of companies making fine glassware and a few are listed here for your convenience. You'll naturally want to see and handle these pieces in a store but these sites will help you find the stores that carry brands you are interested in and may offer online shopping once you decide.

Tableware

You will have no trouble finding almost endless sources of utensils to eat with but I have listed a few sources to help you select your patterns.

www.oneida.com

Stainless steel and silverplate flatware.

www.silversuperstore.com

Hundreds of patterns available at discounted prices from many major manufacturers.

www.siomorfevres.com

Home site of Siom Orefevres.

www.w-right.demon.co.uk

See the designs of W. Wright and Co., Sheffield England cutlery manufacturer.

www.reedandbarton.com

Sterling, silverplate and stainless from Reed & Barton.

www.christofle.com/che11.htm

Christofile allows you to register for fine crystal, linens and flatware at their stores in Paris and around the world.

Tableware

www.yoursilver.com

Discount sterling silverware and stainless flatware.

www.sterlingsource.com

A large sterling silver source.

www.silversuperstore.com

Discount sterling and stainless.

www.braybrook.co.uk

Fine sterling from England

www.flatwarehouse.com

Sterling, silverplate and flatware.

These sites claim to discount the list prices but then again everyone discounts the list prices.

Wedding Etiquette, Traditions and Customs

Every ethnic group has their own wedding customs. The ones you use in your own wedding will probably come from your own background but you will find some fascinating foreign ones listed here and you may want to incorporate pieces of some in your own festivities.

- **www.cftech.com/BrainBank/OTHERREFERENCE/ETIQUETTE/EtiquetteIndex.html**

  Excellent information on etiquette for all phases of your wedding.

- **www.ourmarriage.com/html/ask_fran.html**

  Wedding counselor answers questions about wedding etiquette.

- **www.the-wedding-pages.com/wic/article.html**

  A library of articles on weddings and etiquette.

- **weddingcircle.com/ethnic**

  Customs and traditions in Scottish, Italian and Jewish weddings.

- **www.jmts.com/wedding/customs.htm**

  Fascinating wedding customs from around the world.

The following pages have an extensive list of wedding customs and traditions from around the world which may provide interesting additions to your own wedding.

Throughout history and amongst every people weddings have always held a sacred and prominent position. All of these different traditions make fascinating reading and it's likely you'll find something to enliven your own traditions.

- **melanet.com/awg/**
  African wedding guide.
- **www.acornis.com/india/imystica/vivaha.html**
  Indian wedding customs.
- **www.chcp.org/Vwedding.html**
  Chinese wedding customs.
- **www.weddingguide.co.uk/Traditions.html**
  British and Welsh wedding traditions.
- **www.pbm.com/~lindahl/rialto/wed-trad-FAQ.text**
  Medieval and renaissance wedding traditions.
- **www.acs.ucalgary.ca/~elsegal/Shokel/Weddings_Index.html**
  Jewish wedding traditions.

www.weddingtips.com/wttradit.html

Some wedding traditions and where they originated.

members.aol.com/Mjkarl/ethnic.htm#AMISH

Ethnic wedding traditions from around the world from Amish to Irish to Vietnamese.

www.brideandgroom.com/tradition.htm

A lovely list of the usual time honored wedding traditions.

www.clinique.com/app/nph-wedding.cgi?mode=brided&Host=Clinique

Interesting bridal customs from around the world. In Fiji, for example, the groom presents the bride's father with a whale's tooth, a symbol of wealth.

In some places wedding ceremonies go on for 4 days and among slaves in the U.S. marriage was accomplished by jumping over a broom. Hopefully your ceremony and reception will fall somewhere in between.

There are three types of marriage in Tibet:

1. Monogamy,

2. One husband and multi wives,

3. One wife and multi husbands.

Take your pick.

- **omni.cc.purdue.edu/~wtv/tibet/marriage.html**

  A complete outline of Tibetan marriage customs.

- **www.weddingcircle.com/ethnic/jewish**

  Jewish wedding customs.

- **www.japan-guide.com/e/e2061.html**

  Japanese wedding customs.

- **www.geocities.com/Tokyo/Ginza/9732**

  The (whew) four day Pakistani wedding custom.

- **www.geocities.com/Wellesley/3321/win4a.htm**

  A wonderful outline of Indian arranged marriage customs.

- **www.southmex.com/mexico/traditions/marriagecustoms.html**

  Stealing the bride and other Mexican wedding customs.

Vows and Words

If you would like some ideas and suggestions for designing your ceremony check out these sites.

www.electpress.com/loveandromance/page45.htm

Wedding vow gallery with poems and ideas and links to many sources of vows.

members.aol.com/trevorb1

Personalized wedding vows.

members.aol.com/kshader/zoom7

Wedding vow calligraphy.

www.weddingweb.com/bookstore/vows.htm

Lots of books with wedding vows.

www.Drjohnholleman.com/ma/wed5.htm

Complete Book Of Wedding Vows for sale.

Here are some more sources to help you design and choose wedding vows that are most appropriate for your special day.

- **www.dianewarnerbooks.com/vows.htm**

  There are some ideas here but mostly this is an ad for an entire book on wedding vows.

- **www.freeyellow.com/members2/anilkr/vows.html**

  Some very lovely and original Indian wedding vows.

- **www.stl-online.net/days/vows.html**

  Wedding vows and poems from the soap opera "Days Of Our Lives".

- **library.byu.edu/~rdh/eurodocs/uk/weded.html**

  Sixteenth century wedding ceremony from the prayerbook of Edward VI.

- **members.aol.com/trevorb1**

  Personalized wedding vows for $10.

Wedding Toasts

www.blissezine.com/library/toast_generator.asp

A great wedding toast generator.

www.tmclark.com/JP/toasts.html

A collection of popular wedding toasts.

www.blissezine.com/library/toasts.asp

Bliss wedding magazine gives ideas and tips for toasts and speeches.

www.weddingcircle.com/fyi/speech/speech.htm

An excellent guide to toasts and speeches including great tips on delivery, content and style.

www.thescribbler.com/speechwriter.html

This experienced writer will compose an original speech for you.

www.angelfire.com/ri/tinestb

A customized writing service will create speeches or poems.

www.weddingtoasts.com/intro.html

A resource guide for people who have to speak at a wedding. The book is $9.95 but there are good free tips on the site.

In case the best man or others who are expected to give toasts are a bit tongue tied, nervous or unimaginative you might be able to help them by telling them about these sites that help with toasts.

Honeymoons

Honeymoon Planning

There are endless places to go for your honeymoon and I will try to give you information so you can find most of them. The favorite honeymoon spots have their own pages and give you places to get more specific information. If you are not an experienced traveler it may be easiest to go with a package deal. These can save you money and they take care of all the details and the only down side is that you have less flexibility and choices.

Wherever you decide to honeymoon it's a good idea to let as many people as possible know it's your honeymoon. Airlines and hotels often go out of their way to make your honeymoon special. Wearing bride and groom hats to the airport may get you upgraded and hotels are likely to send a bottle of champagne to your room.

All of the wedding network sites at the beginning of the book offer honeymoon travel. They are usually tied into a travel agency that pays a commission to the site for the referrals. Listed on the next page are some all-inclusive travel sites that provide information on vacation sites worldwide. They are a good source of ideas for places to consider.

All-Inclusive Travel Sites

These sites provide hotel, car rental, airline tickets, vacation packages, cruises and anything else you can think of that involves travel.

www.atevo.com

A well organized travel agency site that gives good information about every location in the world. Just click on "Site Contents" and "Destinations" and pick a country.

expedia.msn.com

Pick a location and they will get you there or introduce you to many packaged tours.

www.thetrip.com

Air, car and hotel booking and if you look further you can find detailed information on every country.

www.4airlines.com

The usual airline, car and hotel reservations but also deals on packages.

www.previewtravel.com/Home

All sorts of destination guides, searches and planners as well as reservation services.

www.atlastravelweb.com/honeymoonpackages.shtml

A quite comprehensive cruise and honeymoon specialist.

Honeymoon Planning Sites

www.honeymoonislands.com
Honeymoon packages for all the favorite sites: Mexico, Hawaii, South Pacific, Caribbean etc.

honeymoons.miningco.com
A very large site that gives you ideas for every possible kind of honeymoon.

www.honeymoonsinc.com
This company specializes in honeymoon travel to Hawaii, Mexico, Caribbean, Disney and features the Sandals resorts.

www.honeymoonsinc.com
They specialize in cruise honeymoons even if they do have an annoying site layout.

travelwat.com/honeymoo.htm
Honeymoon and wedding packages in all the great spots worldwide.

These sites specialize in honeymoons. Most offer package arrangements which may often save you money as well as the hassle of making your own plane, hotel and car reservations. The locations are around the world which will help give you ideas for finding a perfect honeymoon location.

Every travel agent will claim to be a honeymoon expert and perhaps they are. Choose a travel agent who has been around for a while and pay by credit card so you have some redress if the agent or their overseas associates disappear. Look carefully into charter airlines which often do not have the back up of regularly scheduled flights, and into the exact hotel facilities that are offered.

www.4windstravel.com/tours/honey

All inclusive honeymoon planning company that can create just the kind of honeymoon you want.

www.tropicalislandvacation.com

This travel company will customize your honeymoon to any tropical island you have ever heard about.

www.travnavtravel.com

Dream honeymoons to practically every place listed in this book with prices.

www.onlywaytotravel.com/honeymoon.htm

Another travel company specializing in honeymoons of all sorts.

tncweddings.women.com/tc/travel/index.htm

Some very romantic honeymoon vacation ideas.

www.romanticbeginnings.com

Romantic honeymoons from this travel agent who also arranges weddings in these locals.

www.budgettravel.com

Links to all the main worldwide destinations with links to embassies, travel agents, passport requirements, health information, travel by rail, ferry, subway, bus.

www.wtgonline.com/navigate/world.asp

A world travel guide. Just select your destination from the world map and you'll have complete coverage of countries and cities worldwide.

advocacy-net.com/beachmks.htm

A listing of 1,000 beaches.

4honeymoons.4anything.com

Details on honeymoon hotspots around the world.

www.honeymoontravel.com

This travel agent offers discount honeymoon packages to all the famous spots.

www.disneyplace.com

The Disney Resorts information guide.

Be suspicious of deals that sound too good to be true. This is especially important with overseas accommodations whose names you won't recognize and airlines you've never heard of. Check them out independently, if you can, in a travel book.

Discount Travel Sites

If you are an experienced traveler you will probably save money by planning the honeymoon yourself. When going a long distance, the air fare will be a major expense. The variations in air fare are staggering and spending time on these discount sites will save you big bucks. You can't, of course, play games with your honeymoon and take a chance with last minute deals or standby arrangements but there are still amazing prices to be had for air travel and they change by the minute so it pays to snoop around, find out what a very low fare is and then pounce on it when it appears.

www.air-fare.com

Daily update of best available fares.

www.onetravel.com

What you need to stretch your travel dollar.

www.priceline.com

Name your price.

www.cheaptickets.com

More promises of the lowest fares and cruise rates.

www.airdisc.com

Besides low airfares they offer trips to some pretty exotic locations.

www.airhitch.org

Barebones travel to Europe only.

www.aircourier.org

Also known as Cheaptrips.com, "Nobody flies cheaper than our members".

www.frommers.com

Budget travel with Arthur Frommer.

www.lowestfare.com

Hot deals, great vacations, three-day advance purchase airline tickets. It may be useful if you decide to elope.

www.flycheap.com

Fly Smart! Fly cheap!

www.etn.nl

Discount Travel guarantees the internet's lowest fares, or they'll refund the difference.

www.airdiscounter.com

Australian based discount travel site.

www.discount-airfare.com

In winter they show some unbelievable air fares to Europe.

www.lastminute.com

Unbeatable prices on airfare and vacations.

Airline Listings

Airfares can actually change every few minutes and the discount agents listed above can pick these up. If you want to (eventually) speak to a real person, calling the airlines direct gives you this ability and they can provide you with all the detailed information.

www.princeton.edu/Main/air800.html

800 numbers of all airlines with links to many of their sites.

www.period.com/airlines

800 numbers for all airlines.

www.hotelstravel.com/airlines.html

Links to virtually every airline in the world.

www.pathfinder.com/travel/TL/links/airlines2.html

Links to many of the major airlines of the world.

www.airlines.com

Airline search, online reservations, guidebooks, discount travel fares.

Travel Books On-line

- www.fodors.com
- www.frommers.com
- www.lonelyplanet.com
- travel.roughguides.com
- www.wtgonline.com/navigate/world.asp
- www.zagat.com

Once you have decided on a particular honeymoon spot, reading travel books on the place is a very good investment. If you are not buying a packaged tour this is the way to get all the information on weather and places to stay and things to do. Buying 2 or 3 books on your honeymoon choice is a good investment as each book usually gives a different viewpoint. Lonely Planet and The Rough Guides, for example, have a younger more adventuresome and budget minded outlook, while Fodor's and Fielding's tend to emphasize the top of the line places. Parts of these books are available for free online.

Worldwide Health Information and Warnings

If your honeymoon location tends towards the exotic it might be a good idea to check the health and safety of the place. These sites will give you all the scary news.

www.who.int/emc/outbreak_news

Disease outbreak news.

www.cdc.gov/travel

Health requirements and medication recommendations for anywhere in the world.

travel.state.gov/travel_warnings.html

Travel Warnings & Consular Information Sheets.

www.tripprep.com/index.html

Site for general information, health precautions, disease risk summary, official health date, and US advisories.

www.pathfinder.com/travel/TL/links/health.html

Links to multiple health sites. Everything from diving medicine to high altitude sickness.

Cruise and Beach Wear

members.aol.com/jawshawaii

Very sexy bikinis available in all sizes from Hawaii.

dauman.com/swim98/pan1.html

Lots of swimwear from an experienced mail order company.

www.bikini-intl.com

Designer swimwear and accessories.

www.swimsuitsjustforus.com

A terrific swimsuit source for sizes 16 and up.

www.victoriassecret.com/vsc/html/os/swimdex.html

Victoria's Secret swimwear collection.

www.sundancing.com

Swimwear, sarongs and lingerie.

www.chambec.com/ap/suits/index.html

Solar Tan-Thru swimwear.

You can pretty much find warm (and for that matter cold) weather clothes in almost any season but in case you are having difficulty in your area here are a few sites to buy bathing suits and beach wear. For outdoor and ski clothes check page 77.

California Honeymoons

You can find every kind of honeymoon in California. Just ask all the people from around the world you'll find visiting. Take your pick of mountains and oceans and wine country and outrageous cities and charming ones.

gocalif.ca.gov

This is the official State Visitors Guide and it does a beautiful job of introducing you to all the attractions California has to offer honeymooners.

www.californiatraveldreams.com/honeymoons.htm

Some excellent suggestions for specific honeymoons in California.

www.sfguide.com

If San Francisco is on your list this site gives you all the information you could ever need to plan a honeymoon.

www.sonoma.net

Sonoma County wine country is the perfect honeymoon location for wine enthusiasts provided you don't overindulge and fall asleep early every night. This is a terrific site that gives information on everything.

disney.go.com/Disneyland

A complete guide to Disneyland in Anaheim California.

www.sandiego.org

The San Diego Visitors Bureau tells you all about the perfect weather and beaches here. And you can always go to the zoo.

gola.miningco.com

Everything about Los Angeles from accommodations to vices. Great links to hotels throughout California.

www.palm-springs.org

Palm Springs is a desert playground and this site tells you everything about where to stay, eat and what to do.

www.californiatraveldreams.com

A beautiful and complete site on Northern California.

www.monterey.com

The Monterey Peninsular Visitors Bureau tells you all about hotels, attractions and dining plus everything else.

Unless you are staying at a resort you will want a car in California. It's the way California people get around. There is so much beauty to see in between the major attractions, that it would be sad to miss the flexibility to just stop and view.

Florida

Florida is a wonderful honeymoon choice with lots of beaches and probably more theme attractions than any other state. While perfect in the colder months you'll be running to shade in the summer.

- **www.hotelstravel.com/usfl.html**

  Florida State index to hotels and tourist attractions with a city and region breakdown.

- **www.florida-you.com**

  The home page of Florida Magazine.

- **www.fl-travel.com**

  Information on the true Florida.

- **www.2000floridatravel.com**

  The ultimate Florida travel guide.

- **floridatraveler.com**

  Florida travel guide with maps and weather.

- **floridatraveler.com**

  Florida adventure travel guide with things like ballooning, biking, canoeing, etc.

- **www.mytravelguide.com/countries/united_states/florida**

  A comprehensive and detailed resource to Florida travel.

Disneyworld

- **www.disneyworld.com**

  The official web site for Disneyworld information and reservations.

- **www.orlando-hotels-online.com**

  Discount hotels in Orlando near all the attractions.

- **www.freeyellow.com/members6/orlandoairport**

  Tips on flying into Orlando and airport transportation.

- **www.orlando4free.com**

  A discount attraction ticket broker.

- **www.disneytrips.com**

  The unofficial site with great tips for planning your Disneyland vacation.

- **www.wdwinfo.com**

  A Disneyworld information site with discount hotels, weather, etc.

If your parents neglected to take you when you were a kid, make up for it with a Disneyworld honeymoon and don't invite them. Besides the rides there are endless adult attractions. Don't go during school vacations.

Hawaiian Honeymoons

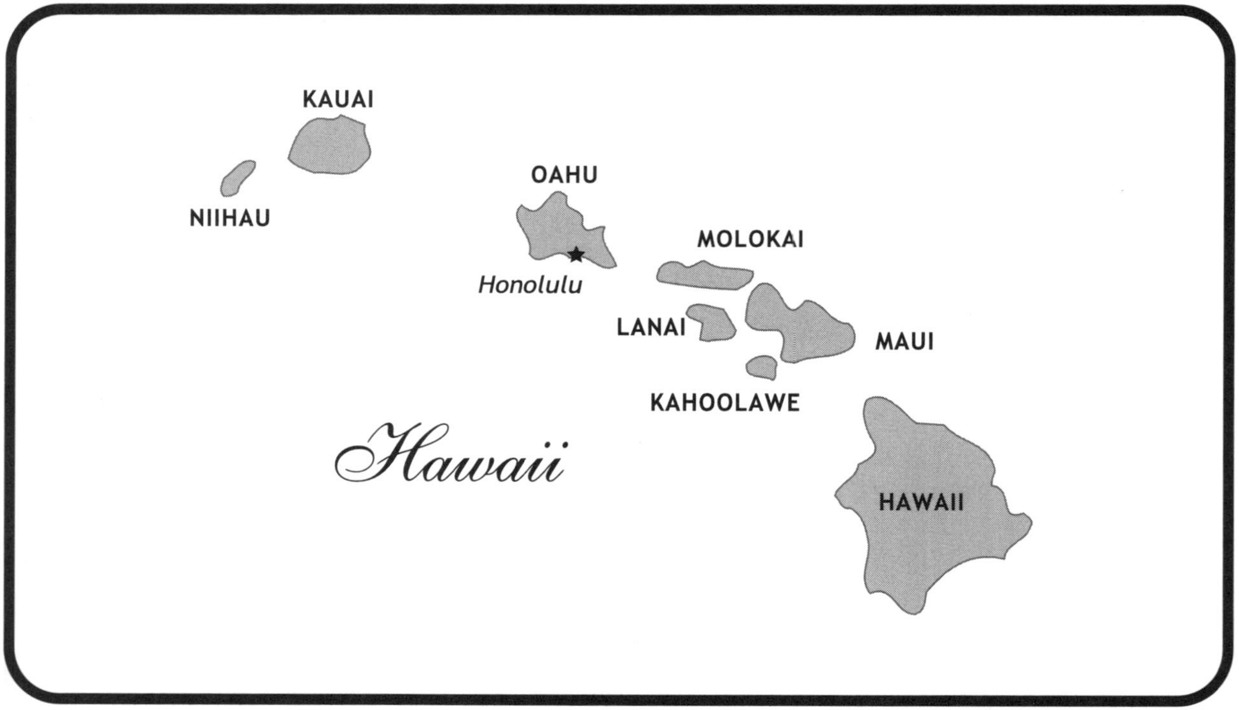

Hawaii has a total of 8 main islands but 5 make up the usual honeymoon destinations.

Hawaii, The Big Island. Over 4,000 square miles and home to an active volcano, pristine rain forests, snow covered mountains, arid desert, beaches and grasslands.

Maui. Desert and rain forests and beaches and highly developed tourist areas on this 726 square mile treasure.

Oahu. The most developed of the islands with the most hotels, restaurants and night life, yet lots of natural beauty if you get away from the main tourist areas.

Kauai. This small island is called the garden island and has fewer tourists and especially beautiful and secluded places.

Molokai. Formerly a leper colony, Molokai is only 261 square miles in size and mostly rural and less touristy.

Lanai. This island is only 13 by 17 miles in size and mostly given to pineapple growing.

Hawaii has it all. Superb weather, easy access, accommodations in all price ranges, magnificent beaches, mountains and landscapes, every kind of food and activities that will wear you out more than you want on a honeymoon.

- **gohawaii.about.com/travel/gohawaii**
  General and specific information about everything Hawaiian. If you read this entire site you'll have no time left to plan your wedding.

- **www.sunfinder.com/oahu.htm**
  A good introduction to Oahu with detailed descriptions, excellent photos, the best hotels, activities weather etc.

- **www.sunfinder.com/maui.htm**
  The same as the above for Maui and the other islands listed below.

- **www.sunfinder.com/hawaii.htm**

- **www.sunfinder.com/kauai.htm**

You will meet lots of other honeymooners and tourists on Oahu and Maui. For seclusion, it's easy to find solitude if you get away from the main hotel areas on these islands. There is no difficulty finding a quiet retreat on one of the lesser developed islands.

www.kauaivisitorsbureau.org

Kauai Visitor Bureau home page.

www.friendlyisle.com

The Molokai web directory with information about the island and excellent photos.

alternative-hawaii.com/special/lanspdx.htm

Information on secluded Lanai as well as all the rest of the islands.

www.visit.hawaii.org

Send for a free 122 page color brochure. Very complete listing of hotels, unfortunately without prices but great activity list.

www.bigisland.org/home.asp

A wonderful site giving historical, cultural and tourist information about the Big Island.

www.gohawaii.com

A very complete resource but lacking prices from the Hawaii Visitors Bureau.

www.alohakauaitours.com

Great Kauai mountain and sea tours for an active honeymoon.

www.bluehawaiiweddings.com/honeymoon.html

Honeymoon packages for all the islands of Hawaii with descriptions and prices.

www.tanega.com/honey.html

Another full service travel agency covering Hawaii and showing lots of prices on their site.

www.theinsider.com/Aloha/index.html

Tips on getting the most out of your Hawaii honeymoon. Loads of information on each island.

www.gorp.com/gorp/resource/US_National_Park/hi_hawai.htm

Adventure activities in Hawaii's National Parks and outdoors.

www.honeymoon-hawaii.com

A Hawaii travel company that specializes in honeymoons. Tons of information on hotels and packaged honeymoons.

travel-hawaii.com

This discount travel agency covers the Hawaiian islands like a blanket and can provide any travel services.

For all its idyllic beauty, petty crime has come to Hawaii in a big way. Don't leave stuff in your car (even in a locked trunk) and secure your valuables at all times.

Massachusetts Honeymoons

There is lots to do and see in this very historic state with the Berkshires for a rural and Boston for an urban honeymoon.

- **www.gorp.com/gorp/location/ma/ma.htm**

  A comprehensive guide to travel and outdoor activities in Massachusetts.

- **www.capecodvisit.com**

  Search engine for Cape Cod, Martha's Vineyard and Nantucket. A visitors information network.

- **www.travelfileaol.com/go/ma.html**

  Massachusetts tourist information.

Cape Cod

The Cape is magnificent in summer but also crowded. The rest of the year you can usually have romantic and secluded beaches and dunes to yourself. Just don't expect to swim without a wet suit.

- **webtravel.org/webtravel/cape-cod.html**

  An excellent Cape Cod guide with descriptions and superb photos of major attractions.

- **www.capecodtravel.com**

  The web version of Cape Cod magazine with links to lodging, dining and things to do.

- **www.pooty.addr.com/listings/Hotels_and_Lodging**

  Cape Cod lodging and hotel index.

- **www.sunsol.com/ccvd**

  The Cape Cod visitors directory with information on everything on the cape.

Martha's Vineyard

- **aoldg.previewtravel.com/DestGuides/0,1208,AWB_339,00.html**
  A destination guide to Martha's Vineyard from Fodor's including maps and weather.
- **www.insiders.com/capecod/main-marthasvineyard2.htm**
  A complete history and tourist guide to Martha's Vineyard.
- **www.mvol.com/places.html**
  Places to stay. Hotels and Bed and Breakfasts.
- **www.mvmainstreet.com**
  Everything about the island from ferries to accommodations to restaurants.

Martha's Vineyard is a 45 minute ferry ride away and leaves you with an "in another world" island feeling. Make reservations in summer if you are bringing your car.

Nantucket

- **www.nantucketonline.com**
  Visit Nantucket online. Lodging, activities, food and more.
- **www.allnantucket.com**
  Nantucket Island information source with links to accommodations, dining and activities.
- **www.maurypeople.com**
  Nantucket beach honeymoon rentals.
- **www.nantucketairlines.com**
  Nantucket Airlines hourly shuttle.
- **www.nantucket.net**
  The official Nantucket Island information source. Events, live cam, weather, events and more.

Nantucket is a 2 and a quarter hour ferry ride and even more secluded in feeling than the rest of the cape. Again, reservations for a car are a must.

Bermuda Honeymoons

Bermuda is a lovely island with pretty scenery and flowers, pink sand beaches, and endless nooks and crannies for honeymooners to explore. It is an orderly, efficient English speaking island that is easy to reach in a few hours by plane from the East Coast of the U.S. Hotels and accommodations are available in all price ranges and visitors travel mainly on motor scooters since no rental cars are allowed. It's small enough so you can explore the whole island in a week and there is enough to do with biking, fishing, diving, sailing, beaching, shopping, golfing to keep you coming back forever.

www.keyguide.com

How to get there, where to stay, what to do and more.

www.bermudatravelnet.com

Extensive Bermuda information source with things to do and wedding and honeymoon information.

www.bermuda.com/info

Complete and comprehensive guide to attractions, beaches, accommodations, dining and all the rest.

www.bermuda.com/info

Bermuda's central reservation service where one phone call does it all.

www.bermudashorts.bm

Lots of pictures of Bermuda along with web cams to whet your appetite.

www.allexperts.com/getExpert.asp?Category=179

Volunteer experts answer your questions about activities, hotels, beaches and whatever.

www.dreamingofbermuda.bm

The most comprehensive links to everything on Bermuda with hundreds of photos.

Mexico Honeymoons

Mexico is an easy drive or quick flight from much of the United States and is a totally enchanting foreign country with a wide diversity of things to see and do. Snow capped volcanoes, beautiful beaches, ancient cities, luxurious resorts and simple local villages all will attract honeymooners. Mexico has a wonderful artistic tradition and cuisine that has been popularized throughout the U.S. and with English widely spoken it is a very easy place to honeymoon. While the cities can be expensive, visiting rural areas can be very cheap.

www.lonelyplanet.com/dest/nam/mexico.htm

Lonely Planet's very complete and comprehensive description of Mexico. A superb site to visit first when planning a trip to Mexico.

www.quicklink.com/mexico/tourist.htm

Travel and tourist information from the Ministry of Tourism. Links to everything you'll ever want to know.

Mexico City may be traffic clogged and polluted but the culture, hotels, food and night life are unbeatable. Snow covered Popocatepetl is only a short drive away where you can get a breath of fresh air.

- **www.go2mexico.com**

  This Mexico travel guide gives the history, weather, health and accommodation information from 15 popular destinations.

- **www.mexicovacations.com**

  A guide to all sorts of accommodations in 9 favorite Mexican locations.

- **www.internationalvacation.com**

  Vacation packages to Mexico and every other honeymoon spot.

- **www.vacation-hotline.com/resorts.htm**

  Detailed packages in Mexico, the Caribbean and other places.

- **www.state.gov/www/regions/ara/bgnpage.html**

  Good background material on Mexico from U.S. Government notes.

- **www.nationalgeographic.com/features/96/mexico/index.html**

  National Geographic gives excellent information on where to go in Mexico with superb photos.

- **www.bestday.com**

  Booking service for hotels and travel in the major resort areas.

- **mexconnect.com/mex_/travel.html**

  Guide to books and links so you can arrange your own trip to Mexico.

- **www.tresmares.com.mx**

  This travel agency specializes in travel to Mexico.

- **www.worldwidevacations.com/honey/mexico/noidx.htm**

  If you are set on a Mexican honeymoon this travel agency makes it very easy.

- **www.excite.com/travel/countries/mexico**

  A very complete Mexico travel site with detailed destinations and weather and the ability to search 5,000 destinations.

- **www.mexconnect.com/index.html**

  The site for Mexico Connect magazine. Articles on the people, food, culture, traditions, art and much more.

Away from the main tourist centers you'll find the people shy yet friendly and if you choose to share their ways your honeymoon will be very inexpensive.

South Pacific Honeymoons

The South Pacific is the magic dream spot of honeymoons. It is also very far away and relatively expensive to get to. I've listed three of the most popular destinations.

Bali

The chaos in Indonesia doesn't seem to affect the mostly Hindu population of Bali. Hoards of Australians vacation there but if you go inland you can get away from the crowds and see some truly beautiful and remarkable cultural things.

www.geocities.com/TheTropics/4414/balen.htm

A good introduction to Bali with history, culture and tourist attractions.

bali-paradise.com/infocenter.html

The Bali tourist information center with information about absolutely everything.

home.mira.net/~wreid

Bali, The Online Travel Guide which is an excellent site with everything you will need to know from weather to dining to hotels.

www.balivillas.com/guide.html

Bali Today, An Insider's Guide. Continually updated information on everything.

www.baliabc.com/honeymoon.html

A Bali honeymoon specialist offering packaged honeymoons.

www.villanet.com/baliring

Click on Index and you'll have almost 50 detailed Bali sites that will give you information on anything you want.

Fiji

- **www.bulafiji.com**

  An excellent overall Fiji Islands travel and accommodation guide from the Visitor's bureau.

- **www.fiji.au.nu/index2.html**

  This travel agency site gives you information on resorts and accommodations throughout the islands.

- **encarta.msn.com/ewa/pages/z/78.htm**

  Fiji Islands weather reports, country profile, Fijian phrase book and much more information.

Not only have they stopped eating each other (and they don't like this joke) but the Fijians are sincerely the friendliest people in the world.

Tahiti

- **www.tahiti.com**

  Island information, weather, hotels, pronunciation guide; just about everything.

- **www.mooreaisland.com**

  Moorea Island is Polynesia's second most popular destination after Tahiti and this site shows you why it is a perfect honeymoon place.

- **www.tahiti-explorer.com/index.html**

  Everything you'd ever need to know about planning a trip to Tahiti.

The bad news is they wear clothes now. The good news is the food is French and the beaches are lovely.

Caribbean Honeymoons

The Caribbean is an easy flight from much of the United States and, with French, British, Dutch and native cultures, offers an amazing diversity of choices amongst extremely well developed tourist facilities.

Antigua

- **www.caribbeansupersite.com/antigua/history.htm**
  A brief history of the Island along with information on beaches and activities, festivals and the like.

- **www.turq.com/antigua/antmap.html**
  Online Tourist Guide with hotel, weather, activities, history and everything else you need to know.

- **www.thetravelsite.com/Dests/DGCarib/gantbarb/eats.html**
  An eating out directory that also has information on all other aspects of Island life.

This low lying formerly British island is 108 Square miles in size and has 356 soft white sand beaches.

Aruba

- **www.interknowledge.com/aruba/anscripts/default.asp?**
  Official Aruba travel guide with loads of information on accommodations, culture, weather, activities and places of interest.

- **www.worldwidemart.com/aruba**
  An engaging history and excellent photos of Aruba.

- **www.lonelyplanet.com/dest/car/graphics/map-aru.htm**
  Lonely Planet's very complete information about everything on the Island.

This happy formerly Dutch Island has luxury hotels on the leeward side and a rugged, deserted surf smashed coast on the windward.

Bahamas

The Bahamas are only 48 miles from Florida, English speaking, and are made up of 16 larger and over 700 mostly uninhabited islands.

- **www.bahama-out-islands.com**

  Travel, history and event information about each of the islands that make up the Bahamas.

- **www.grand-bahama.com**

  What to do and where to stay as well as the Islands' history.

- **2000.bahamas.com**

  The official site of the Government of the Bahamas with information on everything.

Barbados

This former British colony is only 21 by 14 miles in size but boasts one of the best quality of life rankings in the world.

- **barbados.org/visitjrn.htm**

  Visitors' comments and experiences plus information on accommodations, eating, shopping and things to do.

- **www.barbados.org**

  The Barbados Tourism Authority has history and hotels and absolutely everything else you might want to know.

- **barbados2000.com/index.html**

  Complete guide to tourism and culture on the island.

Dominican Republic

www.dominicana.com.do

A complete site (I think) that gets you right in the mood since it is all in Spanish.

www.thebestintheworld.com/dominrep.htm

A travel agency site with good background and weather information and some on accommodations.

www.thedominicanrepublic.net

A complete directory for everything in the Dominican Republic along with historical and background information.

This Spanish speaking country shares the island of Hispanola with Haiti. It is much larger than many other Caribbean Islands with over 1,000 miles of beaches and 8 million inhabitants.

Guadeloupe

194.51.246.27/guadeloupe/p2-in-gb.htm

Sightseeing tours, where to stay, restaurants and everything else you need to know.

www.guadeloupe-fr.com

A very complete site giving information of everything you want to know about the island but all in French. At least it gets you in the mood and you know the food will be great.

www.cieux.com/gdlp.html

The Civilized Explorer's very lovely descriptions of Guadeloupe with great information on restaurants and beaches and loads of pictures.

This French Island about 10 times the size of Washington DC has one of the most beautiful tropical forests in the West Indies and is the center of the Caribbean's Creole culture.

Jamaica

Jamaica is a large 146 mile long English speaking island with 2.5 million people and lovely verdant undulating hills, beaches and waterfalls.

- **www.jamaicatravel.com**
  The official site of the Jamaica Tourist Board with good information on every phase of your honeymoon to the island and even information on how to get married there.

- **www.jamaica-netlink.com/jamaica-netlink**
  A premier source of information about Jamaica with links to everything you'll need.

- **www.jamaica-irie.com/index.html**
  Your source for everything to do. If you check out the Association of Jamaican attractions you'll be too busy to "honeymoon".

Martinique

The beaches and watersports are what bring honeymooners to this French island. It is a fertile, 425 square mile island, large enough to support biking and hiking in the interior.

- **caribbeansupersite.com/martinique/index.htm**
  Good coverage of the history, beaches, watersports and festivals.

- **www.lonelyplanet.com.au/dest/car/mar.htm**
  A super Lonely Planet book description of all phases of life on Martinique.

- **www.frenchcaribbean.com/MartiniqueFrenchCaribbean.html**
  Excellent coverage of accommodations with fine photos of the facilities as well as loads of information on things to do and dining.

St. Lucia

- **www.stluciatravel.com.lc**
  This hotel and tourist association will give you all the information you need about the island.

- **www.stlucia.org**
  St. Lucia's official Tourist Board site and they tell you everything.

- **www.interknowledge.com/st-lucia**
  Lovely photos, nice descriptions, map and vacations details.

This former British colony claims to be the best wedding and honeymoon island in the Caribbean. Three hours from Miami are mountainous hideaways, deserted beaches, and tropical forests.

St. Martin

- **www.st-maarten.com**
  A wonderful description of this tiny island shared by two countries.

- **www.wheretostay.com/islands/islands/stmartin/info.shtml**
  A good island profile, weather and general information as well as a complete list of hotels.

- **www.st-maarten.com**
  The official home page of the St. Maarten (Dutch spelling) Tourist office with loads of everything you'd want to know.

This Dutch-French island lets you mix a Caribbean beach honeymoon with a European ambiance. The island is only 37 square miles with a population of 60,000 people.

U.S. Virgin Islands

The Virgin Islands are made up mainly of St. Croix, St. Thomas, and St. John and are part of America. The 82 square mile island has lovely parks, reefs, rain forests, beaches and old buildings to explore.

www.usvi-info.com

The U. S. Virgin Islands visitor's guide. Good facts but the accommodations and dining are a little skimpy.

www.usvi.net/usvi/stx.html

Excellent photos, listings of activities and accommodations, weather, restaurants and all.

www.virginisles.com

The U.S. Virgin Islands Travel Guide with information on a wide range of island facilities and honeymoons.

Turks and Caicos Islands

This British Crown Colony is made up of 8 main islands covering 193 square miles. Their main attraction is the white sand beaches.

www.interknowledge.com/turks-caicos/index.html

Official site of the Tourist Board with good descriptions and restaurant guide.

www.turksandcaicos.tc

Very complete information on all island facilities down to the local magazine.

www.wherewhenhow.com/Awards.html

A really good site that will give you endless information when you click on a spot.

Canadian Honeymoons

- **www.canadatourism.com/index_ct.html**

  This is the government's travel site and, while not as user friendly as most, it has a tremendous amount of information about all possible honeymoon activities or locations.

- **www.canada.worldweb.com**

  Another country wide planning guide that covers everything with good maps and a very complete list of accommodations throughout Canada.

- **www.discoveralberta.com**

  This is actually the same site as above but the direct route to very complete and detailed information about the province.

- **www.banfflakelouise.com**

  The Banff and Lake Louise area are perhaps the most magnificent in all Canada with stunning alpine beauty and first class honeymoon facilities. This site gives total coverage of the area.

- **bcadventure.com**

  If you are looking for adventure on your honeymoon this site really covers activities in British Columbia. Links to accommodations as well.

Canada is close, convenient and inexpensive with their dollar costing only around 70 cents at time of writing. Everything, of course, costs twice as much so it sort of evens out (just kidding). The Canadian Rocky Mountains are magnificent, the Maritime Provinces remote and enchanting and cities like Quebec a definite European experience.

In the province of Quebec you will really know you are in a foreign country when you find someone actually understands your high school French.

www.tourism-vancouver.org

The official site of tourism in Vancouver which is a lovely city that gets lots of rain. The site gives you total information about Vancouver.

www.travelmanitoba.com

Manitoba seems like an activity kind of place to honeymoon. This site gives all the usual information and has a great opening photo.

www.cybersmith.net/web

New Brunswick claims to have warm water beaches but I'd guess you'd better plan on using them in the summer months. Lots of information here for planning a honeymoon in this province.

www.gov.nf.ca/tourism

The official government site for tourism in Newfoundland and Labrador. It looks like a lovely place to honeymoon but you'd better like snow activities in the winter or be planning to spend the entire honeymoon in bed.

www.destination-ns.com

Nova Scotia is called Canada's ocean playground and this site has every bit of information you might need for planning a honeymoon.

www.tourisme.gouv.qc.ca

Everything you need to plan a honeymoon to Quebec. For accommodations try the next site.

www.quebec-region.cuq.qc.ca

The official site of the Quebec Tourism Bureau with all the lodges, restaurants and activities.

For outdoor lovers there are exciting honeymoon possibilities in Canada's far north. Canoeing, fishing, dog sledding and incredible wild life are all here.

www.nwttravel.nt.ca/

Northwest Territory: For an active honeymoon where you are not going to run into hordes of other honeymooners, this is the place to go.

www.touryukon.com/

Yukon: Untouched wilderness and wildlife on a grand scale.

www.areaguide.net/arctic/

Arctic: There are more hotels here than you would think. Plan on lots of snuggling if you go in winter.

If you are interested in the far north, these three sites give information on the Northwest Territories, Yukon and Canadian Arctic. Bring a double sleeping bag.

Honeymoons in France

French being the language of love it stands to reason that France must be the ideal place for a honeymoon. Just don't expect them to understand your high school French.

- **www.francetourism.com**

  Official web site for the French Government Tourist Office. EVERYTHING!

- **www.france.com/travel/index.html**

  Excellent site for recommendations of hotels, maps, transportation.

- **travel.roughguides.com/content/1830**

  Rough Guide On-line.

- **www.enjoyfrance.com/index.phtml?language=us**

  2000 authentic hotels and guesthouses in France.

- **www.france-random.com**

  Reports and pictures about regions, traditions and products of France. Useful tips (lodging, accommodation, leisure, museums, products).

- **www.omnimap.com/catalog/int/france2.htm**

  List of maps and books available for purchase.

- **www.budgettravel.com/paris.htm**

  Links to embassies, travel agents, passport requirements, health information, travel by rail, ferry, subway, bus.

- **expedia.msn.com/wg/Europe/France/P1574.asp**

  Excellent information on food, arts and culture, types of accommodations, health and safety, transportation.

Paris

A honeymoon in France probably means Paris more than anyplace else. Paris is for lovers and wandering all the romantic places makes for an unforgettable honeymoon.

www.paris-anglo.com/guide/travel/getting/index.html

Here is how to make things easier on arrival in Paris, and how to wander around France and Europe, whatever your budget is.

www.franceguide.com/gb/sejour/index.htm

Sections on things to do and see; sleeping, eating and drinking; places to go, presented by region.

www.discoverfrance.com

Biking tours, getaways, Paris hotels, Paris passes.

www.paris-france.org/pariswe

The city of Paris official web site with beautifully presented information.

www.paris-tourism.com

A great Paris guide with reviews of all the popular places.

www.lonelyplanet.com/dest/eur/par.htm

Lonely Planet's very well written guide to Paris.

www.smartweb.fr

Maps, weather, and all the attractions of Paris.

Honeymoons in Italy

Italy is full of music and romance and warm people. The honeymoon possibilities range from the grandeur of Venice to the beauty of Tuscany to the glory of Rome and everything you might desire in between.

- **www.initaly.com/index.htm**
  In Italy Online - "More information about travelling to Italy than anywhere else on the web."

- **www.lonelyplanet.com/dest/eur/ita.htm**
  Lonely Planet's all inclusive guide to Italy.

- **www2.italy-hotel.com**
  If you know what cities (or region) you will be visiting, this site has a hotel for you!

- **www.budgettravel.com/italy.htm**
  Links to embassies, travel agents, passport requirements, health information, travel by rail, ferry, subway, bus.

- **www.expedia.msn.com/wg/Europe/Italy/P2018.asp**
  Excellent information on food, arts and culture, types of accommodations, health and safety, transportation.

- **www.tripprep.com/index.html**
  Site for general information, health precautions, disease risk summary, official health data, and US advisories.

- **www.travel-italy.com**
  Hotels, Villas, maps, travel information, tours, car reservations.

- **www.italysource.com/travel/travelhome.html**
  Walk in Tuscany, cook in Florence, drive Sicily, ride the rails to Siena & Verona, settle into a villa in Amalfi, cruise the coast from Venice to the Riviera, explore Rome on foot, find your Italian roots.

Italian Cities

Venice

- **www.meetingvenice.it/NewSite/main_en.asp**

  A comprehensive guide to Venice with links to where to stay, what to eat, what to buy, airports, railroads, tourist information, consulates, pharmacies, gondolas, you name it.

- **goeurope.about.com/travel/goeurope/mmore.htm**

  Site for information on Venice including hotels, getting around, practical information, transportation, restaurants.

- **www.worldexecutive.com/cityguides/venice**

  Hotel special offers, luxury hotel accommodation, restaurants, essential travel information and Venice city maps.

> If you want a quiet, secluded Italian honeymoon, Rome and Venice may not be your first picks. They are however, among the most exciting cities in the world.

Rome

- **www.timeout.com/rome/esinf/index.html**

  These pages will give the nuts and bolts info to plan your Roman honeymoon: from banks and emergency phone numbers to handy social tips to help you blend happily into the local scene.

- **www.osinga.com/page.asp?Loc=1708**

  Wonderful details about attractions in Rome plus an excellent list of accommodations.

Ireland Honeymoons

If you are Irish, and just about everyone in the U.S. is, what could be better than a honeymoon to the homeland? Ireland is so green, so friendly and so rich in history and feeling that you'll ignore the questionable weather and lack of warm beaches.

www.touchtel.ie

The premier site to plan and book your honeymoon in Ireland. 11,000 places to stay & 10,000 things to do!

goireland.about.com/travel/goireland

Links to sites for accommodations, specific areas and cities, dining, pubs, and even a site on how to get married in Ireland.

www.budgettravel.com/ireland.htm

Links to embassies, travel agents, passport requirements, health information, travel by rail, ferry, subway, bus.

travel.roughguides.com/content/1830

Rough Guide On-line.

www.golfclubireland.com

Guide to golf courses in Ireland.

expedia.msn.com/wg/Europe/Ireland/P1945.asp

Excellent information on food, arts and culture, types of accommodations, health and safety, transportation.

Greek Honeymoons

Secluded islands with perfect beaches and romantic atmosphere that makes you almost forget the overwhelming historical presence of Greece.

- **www.greektravel.com/index.htm**

  A fun and fabulous site. Matt Barrett's extensive and informative site about Greece. Lots of useful information from a real "insider" point of view. Exceptionally helpful links.

- **expedia.msn.com/wg/Europe/Greece/P1689.asp**

  Excellent site to start your planning. Good, basic information about all phases of your honeymoon.

- **www.greekhotel.com/home.htm**

  Guide to Greek hotels, tour operators, and lodging in Greece. Links to individual islands and cities provide excellent information on general information, history, atmosphere, "don't miss" hotels and agencies.

- **www.travelling.gr/GREECE.html**

  Very hard site to navigate, but full of information. It helps to know exactly what region you wish to visit before using this site. Be forewarned...Athens is "Attica".

- **www.mytravelguide.com/countries/greece**

  All purpose site. Get information, book flights, book hotels, etc.

- **www.vacation.net.gr/p/index2.html**

  Tourist guide of Greece. Sections include: Information by area; The National Tourist Organizational Tips, history and various information; Hotels providing online Reservations; Local Travel Agencies; Adventure Clubs, Medical Centers etc.

Honeymoon Cruises

On a cruise you can take all the incredible luxury right with you as you travel around. You'll be fed beyond belief, probably have lots of activities easily available, and travel to exotic locations. Cruises take lots of the uncertainty out of a honeymoon and will probably bring you home fat, tanned and happy.

www.goawaytravel.com

This travel agency specializes in cruises and will find one for you if you fill out their long questionnaire.

www.mytravelco.com/Cruises

Another cruise specialist but this one does offer a complete listing of cruise lines.

www.captivatingcruises.com

This is a good site that gives comprehensive information on all the cruise lines.

www.traveluniversal.com/Tips.asp

This page has answers to frequently asked questions about cruises and cruise reviews among many other valuable tips.

www.simplycruises.com/honeymoon.html

This company not only specializes in cruises, they can also arrange for you to be married at sea.

www.starwardcruises.com/carn2.htm

The Carnival Cruise Line schedule will give you a good idea of the offerings of a cruise line.

- **www.cruise-source.com/cunard/queenelizabeth2.htm**
  Queen Elizabeth 2 luxury world cruises.

- **www.cruise-source.com/Cruise/crystal**
  An extensive list of cruises all around the world.

- **www.traveluniversal.com**
  This travel company claims to specialize in affordable honeymoon cruises.

- **www.cruisingco.com**
  All the major cruise lines are represented here with detailed listings of their cruises.

- **www.awaytosail.com/index2.html**
  Access to a data base of all major cruise itineraries.

- **www.freecruisequote.com**
  Discount cruises on all major lines. It can't hurt to check out their quotes.

- **cruiseshopping.com**
  Thirty cruise lines and 5,000 cruises. You've got to find what you're looking for here.

The different location and size of your stateroom account for the tremendous range of prices on a ship. As romantically inclined as you are, there is a limit to how much time you'll be spending in your room and this is one place where you can save a lot of money.

Exotic Honeymoon Locations

These sites will lead you to honeymoon places away from the usual ones. The world is full of exciting and remote places and Africa, South America, Asia, and Australia may all be beckoning to you. Off beat places are usually more expensive to get to but the rewards are greater once you arrive.

- **www.aandktours.com/html/index.html**

  Abercrombie and Kents site. Check out the Marco Polo Club for remote and exotic locations.

- **www.lonelyplanet.com/dest/dest.htm**

  Lonely Planet's in-depth descriptions of exotic locations.

- **www.hotwired.com/rough**

  This is the Rough Guide's site which gives information on exotic locations (14,000 they claim) around the world. The information is very detailed and complete.

- **www.africaarchipelago.com/home.html**

  This London agency specializes in travel to East Africa.

- **www.weddingcircle.com/honeymn/asia.htm**

  A zillion honeymoon suggestions in Asia.

- **www.tourism-asia.com/april/tourism_asia_niche_honeymoon.htm**

  Exotic honeymoon spots.

Active Honeymoons

For active couples, especially those who have been living together for 3 years, the idea of a quiet honeymoon vegging out on a beach for a week or two may seem dull. The sites listed here will give you ideas for great active honeymoons that will leave you so tired you'll be happy to come home and just snuggle in each other's arms.

www.gorp.com/akdisc.htm

Alaska adventure trips. White water rafting, hiking, canoeing etc.

www.belize.com/reef%2Dscuba.html

Scuba diving and snorkeling in Belize on their barrier reef.

www.goski.com

Your ski honeymoon site.

courseguide.golfweb.com

While not specifically honeymoons, this is a good guide to golf courses around the world.

www.greatoutdoors.com/index.html

Great outdoor activities of all kinds with links to equipment and ratings.

www.away.com

A travel company that specializes in adventure travel.

Additional Sites

a

b

c

d - e

f

g

h

i - j

l - m

n - o

p - r

s

t

u - z

These humor cartoon books will help you to chuckle your way through all the months of wedding planning. They are all uproariously funny and I'd say that even if I hadn't written them.

The Bachelorette Party #2731
This book explains it all. Who pays and how much to embarrass the bride; arranging transportation and ways to get rid of the "moms". Plus loads of ideas for both pre party activities, like spas, showers and outings and the big event itself.

Great Bachelor Parties #2729
It tells how the best man can organize the best night of his life (well almost) and then gives instructions on damage control if the bride-to-be finds out.

Rules For Engaged Couples # 2730
Rules for keeping weird idiosyncrasies under wraps until after the wedding, registering for cash and handling seating of the family nuts at the reception.

Rules For Sex On Your Wedding Night #2700
Rules if he's a virgin and rules for getting rid of the bellman. Rules for kinky sex and rules for bedroom noise and even rules if you've been living together for 3 years.

Sex And Marriage #2434
What wives really want out of marriage (romance, respect and a Bloomingdale's card); and what husbands want (to be left alone when watching the playoffs and to be allowed to go to bed right after sex)

How To Find A Man And Get Married In 30 Days # 2470
Just in case you really want to get married after reading this book and haven't found Mr. Right.

These books cost $6 each, plus shipping. Just call Sonya at 617-923-1111 to order.